Cosmic Witness

Commentaries On Science/Technology Themes

GEORGE L. MURPHY
LAVONNE ALTHOUSE
RUSSELL WILLIS

CSS Publishing Company, Inc.
Lima, Ohio

COSMIC WITNESS

Copyright © 1996 by
CSS Publishing Company, Inc.
Lima, Ohio

All rights reserved. No part of this publication may be reproduced in any manner whatsoever without prior permission of the publisher, except in the case of brief quotations embodied in critical articles and reviews. Inquiries should be addressed to: Permissions, CSS Publishing Company, Inc., 517 South Main Street, P.O. Box 4503, Lima, Ohio 45802-4503.

Unless otherwise stated, scripture quotations are from the *New Revised Standard Version of the Bible,* copyright 1989, by the Division of Christian Education of the National Council of the Churches of Christ in the USA. Used by permission.

Scripture quotations marked (KJV) are from the *King James Version of the Bible,* in the public domain.

Scripture quotations marked (NEB) are from *The New English Bible.* Copyright (c) the Delegates of the Oxford University Press and the Syndics of the Cambridge University Press, 1961, 1970. Reprinted by permission.

Scripture quotations marked (RSV) are from the *Revised Standard Version of the Bible,* copyrighted 1946, 1952 (c), 1971, 1973, by the Division of Christian Education of the National Council of the Churches of Christ in the USA. Used by permission.

Library of Congress Cataloging-in-Publication Data

Murphy, George L., 1942-
  Cosmic witness : commentaries on science-technology themes / George L. Murphy, LaVonne Althouse, Russell E. Willis.
      p.   cm.
  Includes bibliographical references and index.
  ISBN 0-7880-0724-6
  1. Lectionary preaching. 2. Bible—Homiletic use. 3. Religion and science. 4. Technology—Religious aspects—Christianity. I. Althouse, LaVonne, 1932-   . II. Willis, Russell E., 1955-   . III. Title.
BV4235.L43M87   1996
251—dc20   95-25492
                                                                                          CIP

This book is available in the following formats, listed by ISBN:
0-7880-0724-6 Book
0-7880-0726-2 IBM 3 1/2 computer disk
0-7880-0758-0 Macintosh computer disk

PRINTED IN U.S.A.

To our colleagues in the science-technology work groups of the Evangelical Lutheran Church in America and the United Church of Christ, and the Ecumenical Roundtable on Science and Technology.

Table Of Contents

Introduction	7
Year A	11
Year B	47
Year C	81
Texts Common To Each Year	113
Free Texts	131
Appendices	
A: Index Of Texts By Seasons	139
B: Index Of Texts By Books Of The Bible	157
C: Major Topics And Topical Index	165
D: Technology And Justice	175
E: Story Sermons	177

Introduction

This book is intended as a contribution by the Evangelical Lutheran Church in America's Work Group on Science and Technology, the Working Group on Science and Technology of the United Church of Christ's Board of Homeland Ministries, and the Ecumenical Roundtable on Science and Technology to the Church's ministry of proclamation. The basic assumption underlying it is that the Church is called to preach the gospel in the modern world which is profoundly influenced by science and technology. If this is the case, and if preaching is to be based upon Scripture, then it is important for preachers to discern ways in which Scripture provides resources to address scientific and technological concerns. Our purpose is to help with that work.

The book should be considered a *starting* point for developing sermons which address the intersection of Christian faith and contemporary science and technology. We attempt to raise important questions, introduce and examine crucial issues and ideas, suggest useful illustrations, and entice preachers to consider the challenge of preaching about these contemporary concerns. We have not tried here to develop a unified and comprehensive biblical theology of science and technology. Whether or not such a theology emerges from the commentary as a whole is best left to the reader to decide. While there have, of course, been discussions and correspondence among us, we have not tried to "harmonize" the treatments of the various texts, and it may be obvious where two or three of us have contributed to the discussion of a given pericope. Thus there is an assortment of lenses through which one can view issues of science and technology in the light of the biblical witness. We hope that this variety will be helpful for those who are called to the ministry of proclamation.

Some comments on the role of the preacher may help to indicate the potential we see for such a commentary.[1] The phrase "created co-creator" has been used by Hefner to describe the theological picture of the human.[2] We are creatures, not the Creator, but God has given us the ability to share in the divine creative activity and calls us to use that ability responsibly for the good of the whole creation. The co-creator concept has been used especially in connection with properly informed scientific and technological work. But it is, if anything, even more appropriate for the work of the preacher. For the man or woman who proclaims Christ preaches the creative Word of God, which is identical with the Word through which the universe was created and is sustained (John 1:1-3). From that standpoint, the preacher's work has a good deal in common with the work of the scientist who tries to discern the patterns of creation or the doctor who uses the energies of nature to bring healing. (Cf. Psalm 107:20).

There are, of course, many styles of preaching, many different ways in which the Word can be addressed to people. Some variety in preaching is necessary if it is to have a living character from week to week in a congregation. A lot of things can be excused in a preacher, but being boring is not one of them. Attention to the lessons with which we deal in this commentary will help to correct one potential source of boredom, a tendency of many preachers to focus exclusively on the gospel reading for each Sunday.

Variety in sermon type is also desirable.[3] The traditional *proclamatory* sermon remains indispensable in a scientific-technological age as in less sophisticated periods. Theological treatment of scientific and technological issues will also call for *didactic* sermons — though they should never become simply science or engineering lectures. And the *story* sermon, which has grown in popularity in recent years, can get some new ideas from the genre of science fiction.

We should not give the impression that nothing has been done previously to assist preachers in dealing with scientific and technological issues. Environmental concerns in particular have received plenty of attention by churches in recent years. A recent book by Elizabeth Achtemeier may help clergy to discern possibilities and pitfalls for such preaching.[4]

This commentary is based on texts found in the three-year lectionaries which are now widely used. The texts are listed in the order of *The Revised Common Lectionary* (Consultation on Common Texts, Washington, D.C., 1992).[5] Texts of *Lutheran Book of Worship* (Augsburg, Minneapolis, 1978) are also given. These are denoted by RCL and LBW respectively. When texts are simply given with no indication of a lectionary, RCL and LBW agree. Places where the LBW selection differs, or is found at another place, are noted. In the few cases where an LBW selection is not used anywhere in RCL, it is treated in the position which corresponds most closely to the LBW listing. The readings for "Commemorations" and "Occasions" (with the exception of Thanksgiving, for which RCL provides separate readings for each year) are taken from LBW. Following the pattern of LBW, we have listed Psalms before other readings for each day.

Commentaries on these texts are included in their appropriate seasonal contexts, and these texts have been cross-referenced in Appendices A and B. Other three-year lectionaries are listed as well. Appendix C provides a brief topical index, and Appendix D treats the issue of technology and justice. We have also included a section of commentaries on some "free texts" which are not found in the lectionaries, and have given two science fiction story sermons as examples of this genre.

Texts which seem to have any relevance to theology-science-technology-ethics issues, or are susceptible to illustration from science and technology, have been discussed. At the same time, we have tried to avoid forcing texts in order to discuss them under those rubrics. How often a preacher deals with such concerns will depend on her or his own interests, the nature of the congregation, and current events. Certainly no one should preach about them on every possible occasion, but a significant part of the Church's ministry is being ignored if they are never addressed from the pulpit.

The Bible translation generally used in the commentaries is the New Revised Standard Version, unless otherwise noted. However, texts from the Psalms will often reflect the translation in *Lutheran Book of Worship*, and the verse numbering of the Psalms is that of LBW. Some references are also made to the original languages.

In a few cases we have taken the liberty of extending lectionary readings. Sometimes this simply reflects the fact that traditional selections truncated or omitted the context in which the passage ought to be considered. In other cases the extension reflects the longer texts given in some lectionaries, or the consolidation of one or more listings. Other extensions broaden the scope of passages by including complete chapters or trains of thought.

Endnotes

1. George L. Murphy, "Preaching at the Faith-Science Interface," *Lutheran Partners 10.1*, 1994, p. 14.

2. Philip Hefner, "The Evolution of the Created Co-Creator" in Ted Peters (ed.), *Cosmos as Creation* (Abingdon, Nashville, 1989), p. 211. For further discussion see Philip Hefner, *The Human Factor* (Fortress, Minneapolis, 1993).

3. For the following discussion of types of sermons see Richard A. Jensen, *Telling the Story* (Augsburg, Minneapolis, 1980).

4. Elizabeth Achtemeier, *Nature, God & Pulpit* (Eerdmans, Grand Rapids, MI, 1992).

5. For a brief description of the evolution of the Common Lectionary, and a bibliography of lectionaries, see Peter G. Bower (ed.), *Handbook for the Common Lectionary* (Geneva, Philadelphia, 1987). The full version used here is *The Revised Common Lectionary 1992* (Abingdon, Nashville, 1993). A listing without some of the alternative texts is *The Revised Common Lectionary* (Augsburg Fortress, Minneapolis, 1995).

Year A

1 ADVENT

Isaiah 2:1-5

The first text in the lectionary raises critical issues about the biblical view of technology. God's judgment of the world in "the days to come" is, in part, a judgment on human technology. The text condemns some aspects of the technological ordering of life, but goes beyond that to provide an image of technology in a world ordered by God's will. We are called especially to reflect on the theme of "appropriate technology." Two other themes, "Science, technology, and idolatry" and "Technology and hubris," are suggested by the remainder of the chapter and are discussed at greater length in our selection of Free Texts. For a sermon focusing on technology, the preacher may want to extend the reading for this Sunday to include part or all of verses 6-22.

Verse 4 portrays a new order brought about by divine judgment.

> *They shall beat their swords into plowshares,*
> *and their spears into pruning hooks;*
> *nation shall not lift up sword against nation,*
> *neither shall they learn war anymore.*

God's will for the world is *peace*, and the result of divine judgment and arbitration is peaceful coexistence. There will be no cause for war, and thus no need for its technology. In this refashioned world the instruments of cultivation and nurture replace those of conflict.

While this passage lends itself to sermons on war and peace, the more general theme of appropriate technology can be developed. Isaiah envisions God bringing about a fundamental reordering of the world. Not only will war cease, but all human life, including technology, will be refashioned. Not only will swords be beaten into plowshares, but all technologies for destruction will be transformed into those for life.

The preacher's challenge is to apply this vision to our circumstances, as the prophet meant for it to be applied by the house of Jacob in his own day. We are called to create and use technologies which are just, sustainable, and participatory. (See Appendix D.) Any form of technology might be the focus of a sermon on Isaiah's prophetic vision for appropriate technology. It is not possible to eliminate destruction and waste entirely, for destruction is often a means to new creation and waste is a necessary product of all life. But we are, as much as possible, to redeem technologies of destruction (for example, by using military technology for peaceful purposes) and technologies which produce increasing amounts of waste (by recycling, for instance).

Advent anticipates the *incarnation* of God, God's full revelation in the world. It looks to the coming of the Christ, signaling a new age, and it is an appropriate season for a sermon on technology. Isaiah 2 provides a direct and profound way to talk about incarnation in a technological world. Jesus' birth calls us not only to seek peace instead of war, but to create and use just and sustainable technologies in which all people, not only a trained elite, are able to participate.

God's *shalom* is more than the transformation of technology. The phenomenal claim here is that God's very residence shall be established on the highest mountain in the world: Mount Zion will tower over Everest! All nations will be brought under God's rule through the Law, the gracious gift of God which enables people to live together as neighbors. The Law in their hearts will enable them to act out peace each day as they deal justly and equitably with one another and with creation. To live in *shalom* with nature will mean to conserve, restore, and renew its plant and animal life, its soil, water, air, and other natural resources. Our best scientific and technological resources will be put at the service of the world.

The words of Isaiah 2:2-4 are found again in Micah 4:1-5, which is assigned by LBW as a reading for an Occasional Celebration of Peace. Further discussion, including the issue of "just war," is found there in the section of texts common to each year.

3 ADVENT

Isaiah 35:1-10

The prophet gives hope for exiled Israel, which God has ransomed, to return to Zion. The ways through which they will pass will be renewed — the wilderness will flourish. We have hints of something which will become clear in Second Isaiah, that God's salvation is not just for one nation but all people, and ultimately for the world.[1]

During Advent we prepare to celebrate the coming of One who saves people from their sins. As we await the advent of his righteous rule, our hopes should not be constricted. We do not look for One who will save a few individuals in a narrow "spiritual" sense, but for a Savior who will open the eyes of the blind, give physical strength to the weak, and renew the waste places of the earth. Part of the hope for the coming One is for the environment, for he is the savior of the *world*.

Wilderness and desert should not be thought of only in negative terms. A wilderness can be a place to retreat, to rest, to renew oneself, to recharge spiritually. God found Israel "in a desert land, and in the waste howling wilderness" (Deuteronomy 32:10 KJV), and Jesus and John were formed spiritually in the wilderness. The ecology of the desert is a remarkable part of creation, and the wilderness will not be entirely paved over in God's new creation.

But we know of wildernesses which blight God's world — deserts brought about through careless agricultural practices, dumping of wastes, shortsighted industrial practices, and technological war. The vision of redemption here goes beyond the purely personal to include irrigation of the desert so that it can yield food and beautiful plants, and provide a place for animals to live. This prophecy reverses the story of the Fall. Eden is restored where there now is desert, and all people shall be able to return to Zion on the Royal Highway to be built by God.

The preacher need not leave hopes for renewal of the earth and for healing in the realm of vague generalities or wishful thinking. Some reflection on "good" and "bad" wildernesses, both in the biblical vision and in our understanding of ecology today, could be helpful. And wise uses of today's science and technology can give some illustration of the fulfillment of the hopes which the prophet raises. We now have much greater technological ability to manage the water resources of our planet than did the people of Isaiah's time, and much more effective medical techniques, so that our stewardship opportunities are correspondingly increased. The pictures of healing and irrigation can be expanded to refer to all the scientific, technological, and medical advances that humankind has been given by God. Solar heating, desalinization of water, recycling paper to save earth's forests, and provisions for health care can be part of the fulfillment of this prophecy. Each is a sign that can strengthen weak hands and knees and give courage to fearful hearts. This passage which promises hope also calls us to responsible use of our knowledge and abilities to serve God and God's world.

1 CHRISTMAS

Psalm 148

For this Psalm we can borrow a title from Teilhard de Chardin, *Hymn of the Universe*.[2] The entire cosmos is called to praise God — the heavenly host, the heavens themselves and the earth, living creatures of land, sea, and air, weather, geological features, plants, and human beings of all types. Finally God's people, Israel, is named.

The description of this great choir has some features which we can't accept today in a literal sense. There are no real "waters above the heavens" (cf. Genesis 1:6-8). Elements of an outdated cosmology are used here. But we shouldn't forget the limits of our own models. A hundred years ago scientists thought that there was a peculiar substance, the "luminiferous aether," which permeates all space, including what is called "vacuum," and which serves to transmit light waves. A scientifically literate person of that time might have said, in paraphrasing this Psalm, that the aether vibrates with God's praises. But then Einstein's theory of relativity made the hypothesis of the luminiferous aether as unnecessary as the waters above the firmament.

One might also be concerned about the anthropomorphism of the Psalm. Of course the hills and the creeping things can't sing praises. But human beings can, and the way the Psalm reaches its climax in the praise of humanity indicates that it is this species whose task is to think and to voice the praises of all the earth. Humanity is the universe become conscious of itself and able to speak intelligibly for itself. Relations with the controversial "anthropic principles" of modern cosmology, in which the emergence of intelligent life is seen as a crucial feature of the universe, may be of interest here. (Anthropic principles are considered in connection with Ephesians 1:3-14 for Proper 10 B and Psalm 8 for Trinity C.)

We must see ourselves in a special position in the universe. We can do important things that other creatures cannot do. But we are to do them *for* others. If we are to speak for the sea monsters, fruit trees, and winged birds, we must know them sympathetically, and not merely know *about* them intellectually. (The German language expresses the distinction by using two different words. *Wissen* means to know facts, while *kennen* means to know or recognize a person.)

The fact that the Psalm reaches its conclusion in the praise of Israel is also significant. All people can marvel at the universe itself, but it is those who have been brought to know God through revelation at Sinai and Golgotha who can point humanity to the One who should be praised for creating the world.

Psalm 111 is assigned for this Sunday each year by LBW. We treat it for 4 Epiphany B.

Hebrews 2:10-18 (LBW has this as the Second Lesson for this Sunday in Year C.)

The statement in v. 17 that Christ had to be made like his brothers and sisters in every respect is basic for our understanding of his significance. An axiom which was crucial for determination of some of the christological controversies of the early church was "what has not been assumed has not been healed."[3] That is, God has made possible the redemption of every aspect of proper humanity by assuming it in the Incarnation. The axiom is simply a paraphrase of Hebrews 2:17. (The fact that women as well as men are saved through the Incarnation supports NRSV's inclusive rendering of *tois adelphois* here.)

The thought can be carried even beyond the human race. Romans 8:18-24 and Colossians 1:20 speak of the salvation of all creatures through the Incarnation. But if "what has not been assumed has not been healed," that can only take place through the assumption of nonhuman creatures by the Word. And that is just what evolutionary theory suggests. We all carry in our bodies connections with living creatures, our anatomical and biochemical constituents, our genetic code, our embryological development and our common history. In becoming human, the Son of God took on those relationships as well, becoming like us a distant cousin of dogs and cats and dinosaurs. It is, of course, scandalous to think of God sharing those relationships, but that is the same as the scandal of God born in a stable and dying on a cross.[4] It is like a strong person lifting a great load, who has to get all the way under it to raise it up.

1 EPIPHANY (The Baptism of our Lord)

Isaiah 42:1-9 (LBW has vv. 1-7 for all three years.)

God who sends the servant/ruler Messiah identifies Godself as the Creator of heaven and earth and "what comes from it." It is this God who also (v. 6) has called *you* in righteousness, taken *you* by the hand, kept *you* and given *you* as a covenant to the people and a light to the nations. When Second Isaiah was written, the covenant people was exiled Israel. Today it could be a congregation, a scientific community, any group hearing the call to peace, justice, conservation and renewal of creation. In times of personal confrontation with responsibility, it could be an individual.

Your task, communal or individual, takes shape in light of the calling of the servant/ruler who is your leader, savior, and teacher. Employment of scientific and technical knowledge and deployment and allocation of resources must be considered in this cosmic context.

2 EPIPHANY

Isaiah 49:1-7 (LBW has vv. 1-6.)

God makes exiled Israel "a light to the nations, that my salvation may reach to the end of the earth." God gives an exiled and enslaved people a mission, to bring the story of the mighty acts of God to all nations and to invite them to become God's people. The New Testament sees the Israelite Jesus as the fulfillment of that promise (John 8:12), and his disciples as those who carry on the mission (Matthew 5:14) to make God's salvation known. This includes a call to place all knowledge in God's service. We are called to bring a world gifted with scientific and technological understanding to an awareness of God's authority. When people gifted with science and technology come to an awareness of the gospel, their scientific work can gain new meaning, and they can look toward responsible use of their gifts in the service of God and for the benefit for humankind.

4 EPIPHANY

1 Corinthians 1:18-31 (LBW has vv. 26-31.)

The natural way for people to think about the universe is to imagine that the earth is at its center, and that the sun and everything else move around us. That's the way almost everyone saw things until the Polish astronomer and priest Copernicus in the sixteenth century suggested the wild and crazy idea that the earth and other planets moved around the sun. It went against common sense but it was true, and it changed the way people thought about the universe.

A traditional way for people to think about God is as the absolute, unchangeable One off in heaven, who can't really be affected by anything that happens in the world. Paul tells the Corinthians that that is not where to look for the meaning of reality. Though the cross of Christ is foolish and scandalous, the crucified Son is the center of the universe. He is the Wisdom of God (v. 30). Christian thought has too often drifted back to old-fashioned ideas of God as the impassible Absolute.

Evangelical preaching should call the Church always to the "Copernican revolution" which Paul proclaimed: the crucified Son is the center. And the way in which Copernicus brought about a radical change in our view of the world, from common sense to the "scandal" of a moving earth, can be used to illustrate the new way in which the world is seen when the cross is at its center.

There is another way to illustrate this point. In science one must begin with some assumptions. The assumptions of classical physics, such as that time passes at the same rate for everyone, were essentially common sense. With them, scientists like Newton were able to make progress toward understanding the world. But it eventually became clear that common sense was too simple. Scientists were driven to abandon common sense and to explore the implications of apparently crazy — but true — ideas like the relativity of time. In a similar way, Paul tells us that we can only begin to grasp God's relationship with the world if we begin from the crazy idea that God is revealed to us in the cross of Christ.

5 EPIPHANY

1 Corinthians 2:1-12 [13-16] (LBW has vv. 1-5.)

There is a strong wisdom tradition in the Old Testament and the Apocrypha. "Wisdom" is the biblical concept which best corresponds to today's idea of science. Through wisdom, people can understand and control the world. But we know all too well that knowledge and control are not always used "wisely." Scientific understanding and technological power don't assure ethical behavior. That is why the wisdom tradition continually insists (Job 28:28, Psalm 111:10, Proverbs 1:7, 9:10 and 15:33, Sirach 1:14) that true wisdom begins with the fear of God. And to the Corinthians, some of whom were very proud of their "knowledge," Paul insisted that in order to be wise in the deepest sense, one has to begin with "Jesus Christ, and him crucified," for he is the true Wisdom of God (1 Corinthians 1:31).

6 EPIPHANY

Deuteronomy 30:15-20

In his book *The Strange Story of the Quantum*, Einstein's onetime co-worker Banesh Hoffmann used verses 15 and 19 from this passage to conclude his chapter on the developments in nuclear physics which led to the atomic bomb.[5] We might be tempted to accuse him of taking those words out of context. This chapter of Deuteronomy is, after all, supposed to be a speech of Moses reminding Israel of the threats and promises in God's law.

Perhaps Hoffmann wasn't so far off. God has created the world so that it operates in accord with definite laws. That is a blessing, for it allows us to make sense of the world of which we are part.

It also means that our actions have consequences. If we use nuclear energy or any other discovery unwisely, we and our world will suffer for it. No, God will not rain miraculous fire from heaven on us. We'll do that ourselves! Judgment will be expressed by God's letting it happen. Our punishment will be the consequence of our actions.

That can be the result if we "serve other gods" — whether the gods of the Canaanites or our own technology. If we "love the LORD [our] God, walking in his ways," then we will see the energies of nature as creatures of God and try to use them in accord with God's will.

8 EPIPHANY

Matthew 6:24-34

People often see the need for science and theology to interact with one another in discussions of the origins of the universe. It is well to remember that in his explanation of the First Article in *The Small Catechism*, Luther focuses on God's provision of the necessities of life for us *today*. We understand in scientific terms a great deal about how the grass grows and the birds get food. The doctrine of creation says that it is the heavenly Father Jesus speaks of, working through natural processes, who provides food for the birds and for us.

This text is also a two-sided promise about God's faithfulness. Since God works through natural processes, scientific and technological advances are God's gifts. We are to acknowledge the Creator as the source of knowledge and discoveries, and even of the capacity to know and discover. At the same time, we are called to examine the uses of our knowledge in order to serve humanity and creation in ways which affirm and witness to God's intimate care for all creatures. We too are to care for the birds as well as for human beings.

TRANSFIGURATION

2 Peter 1:16-21

Astrology is big business; many people consult their horoscopes to determine how they should live. Astrology looks scientific as it talks about the positions of stars and planets and the way they're supposed to influence us. Alas, it doesn't work. As a means of telling about real life, astrology is a fraud. You can't get that kind of information from the stars.

But astronomers can get more subtle information by studying the stars, information about the basic forces and elements of the universe. And, rarely, a brilliant exploding star called a supernova bursts into view, providing scientists with a gold mine of information about reality. (The 1987 supernova in the Small Magellanic Cloud was seen just a few days before this text came up in the lectionary that year. Sermon illustrations aren't always that timely, but the newspapers continue to run horoscopes, and astronomical discoveries with the Hubble Space Telescope and other instruments often make the news. The preacher should not have to stretch things too much to develop an illustration.) The contrast between true and false knowledge, between "cleverly devised myths" and the Morning Star to which the prophets and apostles testify, can be clarified by analogy with the contrast between astrology and astronomy.

1 LENT

Genesis 2:15-17; 3:1-7 (LBW includes 2:7-9, to which some of the following comments refer.)

The first part of this passage speaks of God's creating humanity "from the dust of the ground." That is, in the realistic Hebrew view, what we are, a view with which modern biology agrees. We aren't composed of any special "vital" substance, but of the same carbon, nitrogen, and other elements as earthly minerals. We share with other animals this characteristic of being dust into which God has breathed (Psalm 104:29).

We are also set apart. God has made us able to hear and respond to his Word, and thus to be in conscious fellowship with our creator. It is only when humanity chooses to listen to another voice that "dust" becomes a word of judgment, as we hear every Ash Wednesday: "Remember that you are dust, and to dust you shall return" (Genesis 3:19).

In verse 15, humanity is placed in God's garden to "till" (or "serve") and "keep" it. These same Hebrew verbs, *'abad* and *shamar,* are used in the Book of Numbers (3:7, 8; 4:47; 16:9) to describe the duties of those who are to care for God's sanctuary, the tent of meeting, in the wilderness. This suggests that humanity's task of caring for the earth should be seen as a sacred duty of serving God's temple. The naming of the animals in vv. 19-20 (omitted in the lectionary) is also part of the theme of humanity's special privileges and responsibilities.

The ancient Hebrews would have recognized tilling and keeping the garden as technological terms, for agriculture was, by that time, a technological feat. Thus the God-decreed human vocation would not have been a romanticized view of "natural" life, but of purposeful, technologically augmented work. This technological vocation needs to be considered as part of the human responsibility to participate with God as one created in the image and likeness of God, one of the themes of the first chapter of Genesis. (See the commentaries on Genesis 1:1—2:4a for Trinity A and Matthew 13:31-33, 44-52 for Proper 12 A.)

The human calling is to be exercised within clear limits, symbolized by the prohibition placed upon the eating of certain fruits. There are parameters established by God within which human authority is to be exercised. From the whole biblical story which begins in these early chapters of Genesis, we can set out some of those parameters:

1) A call to place all our abilities in God's service;
2) A concern for justice for all, but especially for those least able to secure it for themselves;
3) A concern to liberate all life from oppression;
4) God's amazing grace which always forgives sin.

Within this context, a preacher can look at specific responsibilities for science and technology of concern to the parish in which he or she is proclaiming the Word.

Romans 5:12-19 is discussed for Proper 6 A.

Matthew 4:1-11

The tests of God's Son at the beginning of his ministry are the same as those of Israel, God's "first born son" (Exodus 4:22-23) in the wilderness. The three temptations and Jesus' response to them come from Deuteronomy. But there is a difference: Israel failed the tests, while Jesus succeeds through his trust in God.

Jesus, in other words, "recapitulates" Israel's history, repeating and doing rightly what God's people had failed to do. (Cf. also the use of Hosea 11:1 in Matthew 2:15.) Irenaeus spoke of Jesus passing through all the stages of human life to sanctify them. In the nineteenth century the German biologist Haeckel developed the idea of embryological recapitulation as an argument for evolution. (Today we know that a human embryo does not literally go through the forms of its adult ancestors, but at certain stages it does show close similarities to the embryos of other species to which we are related.) The theological concept can be connected with the evolutionary one: by taking on human nature in the Incarnation, God shares (as each human being does) in the evolutionary history of humanity. Thus in the Incarnation God assumes not only humanity but, in a real sense, the entire biosphere. This gives vivid insight into the way in which Christ can be the savior not just of human beings but of the *world*.

(For further discussion see the corresponding Sunday for Year B. The recapitulation theme suggested by Mark's temptation story is different and more directly applicable to evolution.)

2 LENT

Psalm 121 is the RCL selection. See the discussion for Proper 24 C.

4 LENT

John 9:1-41 (LBW has this for 3 Lent.)

The presence of what has been called "natural evil" in the world is obvious. People have accidents and get sick. This seems to be a necessary part of finite existence, a consequence of God's creating a world which operates in accord with rational laws. As far back as the Book of Job, natural calamities have challenged belief in a beneficent God. Preachers will be wise to address such concerns which some of their hearers are likely to have, even if it isn't always possible to offer comfortable solutions.

The lawfulness of the world is a great blessing. It would be negated if God intervened miraculously every time someone got in trouble. People often try to find the source of natural evils such as illness in *moral* evils of specific persons, as Jesus' disciples do at the beginning of this story. But Jesus denies the premise: you can't always blame natural evil on sin. Jesus doesn't attempt to explain the origin of evil, but says that God is going to be glorified by bringing good out of evil.

5 EASTER

Psalm 33:1-11 is the LBW Psalm for this Sunday. See the commentary for Proper 14 C.

John 14:1-14 (LBW has vv. 1-12.)

Jesus says here that he is "the real and living way" (Moffat), and that "no one comes to the Father except through me." One might think this means that a person can get only part of the way to God without Jesus. But his statement is a qualitative, not a quantitative, one. You can't even get close to God except by him. When you've done all the climbing toward God that you can under your own power, God is still just as far away as at the beginning.

That is not common sense, but it can be illustrated with an example from modern physics. Suppose a ray of light is speeding away from you at the speed of light, which has been measured to be 300,000 kilometers per second. It seems only common sense that if you run after it at half that speed, it will be moving away only half as fast, and that you can catch up with light if you run fast enough. But as Einstein first realized, common sense is wrong here. He argued that no matter how fast you chase a ray of light, it will still be speeding away from you at 300,000 kilometers per second. Experiments have shown that Einstein was right. The speed of light is a physical absolute, and you can't catch up with light.

6 EASTER

Acts 17:22-31

Paul's Areopagus speech is important for the question of "natural theology," an important one for the relationship between science and Christianity. Can there be a natural theology prior to the specifically Christian message which can serve as a preparation for the gospel? Or was Karl Barth right in rejecting such a possibility? Paul's argument might suggest the first alternative, but it should be remembered that *we* have this argument only in the context of the Book of Acts which begins with the gospel.

The unknown God of whom Paul speaks is just that — *unknown* — until Paul proclaims him to the Athenians. And Paul quickly moves to the resurrection of Jesus as the heart of his message. (Verse 18 indicates that some casual listeners thought that Paul was proclaiming another god, *Anastasis,* along with Jesus.)

Preachers and teachers need to be careful about the use of natural theology arguments. "The world is so beautifully ordered! How could anyone *not* believe in God?" It is very easy — indeed "natural" — for some people to come to rest in the kind of religion engendered by such arguments, a theology of glory rather than a theology of the cross. But it is, as the great mathematician Pascal said, "the God of Abraham, Isaac, and Jacob, the God of Jesus Christ" who is to be preached, not simply "the God of the philosophers."

PENTECOST

Psalm 104:25-35, 37 (LBW has vv. 25-34.)

Though it is a little long, it would be good to use the entire Psalm, one of Scripture's great hymns to the creator. God is praised for having created the earth in the beginning *and* for providing for all the creatures of the world, including human beings, today. God's creative work is not to be limited to the past or to the present.

Of special significance is the fact that God's providence for humans is part of God's care for all living creatures. We are together with the wild goats, the birds, the lions, and Leviathan. Humanity does have a special role: it is, after all, a human being who is able to praise God with these words! But we cannot separate the verses which refer here to humanity from those which speak of the rest of the world. This is especially clear in vv. 30-31, where all living creatures live because God gives them "breath." All life comes to be and is sustained through the Spirit of God, who is called "Lord and giver of life" in the Nicene Creed.

Verse 36, in which the psalmist asks God to destroy sinners, seems to end the Psalm on a jarring note. It may be helpful to recall a story about Abraham Lincoln. Someone criticized him for being too lenient to his enemies. "You shouldn't try to befriend your enemies," he said. "You should destroy them." Lincoln replied, "When I make an enemy my friend, am I not destroying my enemy?"

TRINITY

Genesis 1:1—2:4a (LBW concludes with 2:3.)

This opening passage of the Bible offers many possibilities for proclamation and teaching about God as the creator. Here we note a few points which are significant for the contact between science and faith.

Our text is a theological and perhaps liturgical account of the creation of the world by the God of Israel, with some polemic against pagan views. It is not the type of account one might find in the notebook of a scientific observer of natural phenomena. (That is strongly suggested by *internal* evidence, such as the fact that both this and the second creation account, Genesis 2:4b-25, cannot *both* be chronicle-like accounts.) The basic question for Christians is not the *truth* of the account but that of determining what *kind* of account it is. A great deal of supposed conflict between science and the Bible arises from a failure to make this distinction properly.

Such ideas are familiar to many preachers, but will not be so familiar to many people in the pews. Such reconciliation as has taken place for them may have been in terms of rather loose ideas about "myth," or by stretching the creation days to make room for the billions of years called for by science. Pastors have a responsibility to help people understand the character of the Genesis accounts as authoritative but not simply history "as it really happened." When that is done, both Scripture and science can carry their full weight in our discussion of origins.

An important aspect of the text is the *mediated* creation of life. God does not simply make living creatures from nothing but, in vv. 11-12, 20-21, and 24-25, commands the waters and the earth to bring forth life. The material of the world is able to bring forth life when God wants it to, as Gregory of Nyssa and many other fathers of the Church realized.[6] (Note also that in v. 21 this action is described with the Hebrew verb *br'*, God's exclusive prerogative of creation.) The text is thus open to an evolutionary understanding of the development of life. For that matter, it is possible that the entire development of the material universe, back to the first instant of the big bang, can be explained scientifically in terms of natural processes, while it remains a work of divine creation.

In vv. 26-28 God gives humankind, male and female, "dominion" over the earth. It has been argued that our present ecological crisis has its roots here in the idea that humanity is to rule the earth and other living creatures, using them for our own benefit.[7] We have to admit that such misunderstanding of Genesis has to bear part of the responsibility for our environmental problems.

But that idea of "dominion" *is* a misunderstanding. In the text itself, dominion is, in part, an explanation of what it means for humanity to be created in the image and likeness of God. We are to rule the earth as God's representative, *as God rules.* And God's rule is not one of ruthless self-interest, but of love, care, and self-giving for the whole creation. We see that, for example, in Psalm 145, and most clearly in the Christ-hymn of Philippians 2:5-11. For a proper understanding of the dominion we are called to exercise, we must look to Christ who is "the image of the invisible God" (Colossians 1:15).

Many different conceptions of the human vocation have been developed in Christian theology to explain and describe the human role as God's representative, created in the image and likeness of God. These concepts range from notions of co-creation to stewardship and servanthood. Each of these metaphors of the human vocation suggests *some* level of human participation. The question is what kind and degree of human participation is willed by God.

With the emergence of human genetic manipulation, the debate over which of these metaphors is theologically viable, or how they might be combined, will no doubt intensify.[8] This passage invites the preacher to explore these metaphors in the light of emerging science and the ongoing theological debate.

PROPER 5

Psalm 33:1-12 is given as an alternative by RCL. For discussion see Proper 14 C.

PROPER 6

Romans 5:1-15 (RCL has vv. 1-8. LBW has vv. 6-11 for 4 Pentecost and vv. 12-15 for 5 Pentecost.)

One real problem which evolution poses for theology (to be distinguished from many pseudo-problems which people have fought over) is how to understand the presence of death in the world for millions of years before human beings came on the scene. A traditional maximal western view of the impact of original sin was that the death of all creatures was a result of Adam's fall. Such a straightforward casual understanding is not possible if many generations of nonhuman creatures had already died. Furthermore, the Darwinian idea of natural selection even sees death as an essential factor in the evolution of life. Romans 5, a critical chapter for the history of the doctrine of original sin, gives us an opportunity to think about this issue.

The verses which speak of Adam's sin and its consequences have to be seen in the context of the preceding and following verses about Christ. Christ is not merely a corrective for a mistake which humanity made. It is Jesus, not the first human beings (about whom the Bible really says very little, and from whose remains science can elicit little for our ethical guidance), who shows us genuine humanity. Barth emphasized this when he titled his book on this chapter not *Adam and Christ* but *Christ and Adam*.[9]

Augustine thought that original sin was transmitted to the child through the sexual act, but the idea that it has such a *genetic* character is difficult for us to make sense of today. (It also lacks scriptural basis, unless one forces Psalm 51:6.) It may be more helpful to use an *ecological* metaphor. We cannot fully understand living organisms without their environment, and we cannot fully understand a human being except as part of the whole human community. This is true even — or perhaps especially — before birth. And the problem is that we are conceived and born in a human environment in which sin is unavoidable. We participate from the start in an ecology of sin.

What about the idea that death was caused by the first sin? The existence of sin, of separation from God, casts a different light on death, including death that took place *before* there was sin. Now it is seen as something more than, something worse than, the stopping of biological machinery. The *meaning* of death has been changed by sin.

PROPER 8

Psalm 89 is given as an alternative by RCL. For discussion see 4 Advent B.

PROPER 9

Zechariah 9:9-12 (For 7 Pentecost in LBW.)

The Israelites had a tradition of warfare from their time in the wilderness, but it was not technologically sophisticated. They did not have iron or use war horses and chariots as the Canaanites did. (See, e.g., Judges 4:2 and 1 Samuel 13:19-22.) These state-of-the-art items of military hardware thus became for Israel a symbol of alien pagan culture. And under the monarchy, when Israel and Judah themselves had such weaponry, the prophets could use it as a symbol of idolatrous dependence for security on something other than the God of Israel.

Some issues of peace and war are the same for us as they were for people thousands of years ago, but the role of technology in warfare has greatly intensified. It can be very tempting to think that technologically sophisticated weapons systems guarantee security, and therefore to trust them for prosperity and peace. But such uses of technology can provide at best a penultimate security. It is the King who comes to Zion on Palm Sunday, riding a donkey on his way to the cross, who brings real peace and freedom.

We might go on to include the idolatry of technology and science in general. To what degree does our culture "bow down" to scientifically-based high technology? To what degree do we place our hopes for security on technological fixes (either actual ones or those we simply wish we had) for the difficult social and environmental problems of our time? To what degree have we allowed science to become the final authority, even in questions of ethics and faith? (See the discussion of Isaiah 2:6-22 in the Free Text section.)

PROPER 10

Isaiah 55:10-13 (LBW has vv. 10-11 for 8 Pentecost.)

God's Word will accomplish God's purpose with a certainty with which only the certainty of natural process operating in accord with rational laws can be compared. In fact, those laws can be seen as an expression of that same Word — the creative "Word of the LORD" which called the world into being and which came to the prophets, the *logos* of the universe who is incarnate in Jesus and present in the live proclamation of the gospel.

Psalm 65:1-13 is given as an alternative by RCL. For discussion see Harvest in the texts common to each year.

PROPER 11

Isaiah 44:6-8 (LBW for 9 Pentecost.)

The prophet calls God "the first and the last," an expression picked up in the Book of Revelation to speak of God and Christ (Revelation 1:8, 11; 22:13). The parallel phrase from Revelation, "Alpha and Omega," was used by Teilhard de Chardin when he designated the future convergence of the universe as the "Omega Point" toward which the evolutionary process points, the Christ in whom the whole universe will find its fulfillment.

Often evolution is spoken of in the Church only as a *problem* having to do with what took place in the past. Preachers who have no problem with evolution as a biological theory may avoid any mention of it in sermons for fear of stirring up trouble. That is probably a mistake. Teilhard reminds us that we also have the opportunity to speak about the evolutionary process as one of the means through which God will bring about his ultimate future, Omega — Christ.

Romans 8:12-25 (LBW has vv. 18-25 for 8 Pentecost.)

For Augustine, Luther, Wesley, Barth and others, Paul's letter to the Romans is the great manifesto which proclaims God's gracious salvation of the sinner. And it is even more. The present verses speak of God's liberation of the entire creation.

Unfortunately some theologians, whose existential view of Christianity has little place for the nonhuman part of creation, downplay the cosmic significance of this passage. But Paul does have a cosmic view here. "The creation" in v. 22 corresponds to "all things" in Colossians 1:20. Of course there is a difference for theology between human beings and other creatures. The creation looks for the manifestation of God's children as a fundamental part of its liberation. The theme of the earlier chapters of Romans, the justification of the ungodly by God's free gift in Jesus Christ, is the basis for hope in our text. The liberation of the whole creation takes place through Jesus, for in becoming human, God has (through our evolutionary relationships with other living things) come into an organic association with the world.

The promise here is that the creation will be freed from its "bondage to decay." Corruption, the "coming apart" of things because of their time-bound character, was a basic problem for early Christian writers and their non-Christian contemporaries. The work of Christ was seen as liberation from the corruption associated with death. (That is why incorruptibility of the body after death has been seen, especially in the Roman and Orthodox traditions, as a sign of special sanctity: see Acts 2:31 and Dostoyevsky's use of the theme in *The Brothers Karamazov*.)

Today we describe the tendency toward decay with the Second Law of Thermodynamics, which limits the extent to which heat can be converted to useful work. At the microscopic level this is due to the tendency of molecules to move toward more probable, and thus less ordered, distributions, and so has been called "the law of increasing disorder." The Second Law is a fundamental part of the scientific understanding of the world. Though it is statistical in nature, the "law of large numbers" gives it a compelling character when it is applied to systems containing many molecules. The material world thus seems doomed to decay.

But that is not the whole story. Scientific work in recent years has shown that, even in systems in which energy is being dissipated as the Second Law demands, ordered patterns called "dissipative structures" may develop. The "convection cells" which can form when heat flows through a layer of fluid are an example. We are very familiar with one important type of dissipative structure — life! Living systems, through which a flow of energy takes place, are ordered structures which can be maintained for a while against the general tendency to decay.

That does not, in itself, mean freedom from decay. Life does, after all, eventually come to an end. The hope offered in Romans 8 comes about through God's entrance into our world of becoming and passing away. As a participant in the suffering and dying of our existence, the eternal God brings the possibility of a new creation in spite of suffering and death.

The Body of Christ (Romans 12:4-5) is the ultimate "dissipative structure" which is to be the nucleus for the liberation of the world.

With freedom comes responsibility. As Christians even now participate to some degree in the freedom promised for creation, they are called to use their scientific and technological abilities to further God's ongoing redemptive work.

PROPER 12

1 Kings 3:5-12 (LBW for 10 Pentecost.)

Because God gave Solomon the gift of wisdom he became the wisest person of his time, and great wealth and power came to him. In Jewish and Islamic traditions, Solomon had magical abilities to control the powers of the world. (That is supposed to be how he was able to carry out the engineering feats for the construction of the Temple.) But a later chapter of 1 Kings tells how Solomon, for all his understanding, committed idolatry and "his heart was not true to the LORD his God" (1 Kings 11:4) who had given him wisdom. So his great empire came apart after his death and the people of God were split.

In Friedrich Dürrenmatt's play *The Physicists,* it is "poor King Solomon" who represents the modern scientists whose work has the potential to destroy the world. His closing speech sets out the dangers of merely worldly wisdom:

> *I am Solomon. I am poor King Solomon. Once I was immeasurably rich, wise, and God-fearing. The mighty trembled at my word. I was a Prince of Peace, a Prince of Justice. But my wisdom destroyed the fear of God, and when I no longer feared God my wisdom destroyed my wealth. Now the cities over which I ruled are dead, the Kingdom that was given unto my keeping is deserted: only a blue shimmering wilderness. And somewhere round a small, yellow, nameless star there circles, pointlessly, everlastingly, the radioactive earth. I am Solomon. I am Solomon. I am Solomon. I am poor King Solomon.*[10]

This text provides an opportunity to speak in a balanced way about dangers of science and technology. They are not activities which are evil in themselves, but they can become threats when they are divorced from "the fear of God" and regarded as ends in themselves.

Matthew 13:31-33, 44-52 (LBW has vv. 44-52 for 10 Pentecost.)

Verses 44-52 are also given by the *Lutheran Book of Worship* for the commemoration of "Artists and Scientists" and (beginning with v. 47) for "Theologians." The final two verses are the key for all those callings in God's service. Great scientists know the work of their predecessors, respect it, and make use of it. (No competent physicist would speak sneeringly of the work of Newton, in spite of the serious limitations of his theories.) But that does not mean that we are constrained by ideas of the past. The creative artist or scientist or theologian is able to bring forth something really new. This can be seen as an expression of the belief that humanity was created "in the image and likeness of God," so that the human is, in Philip Hefner's phrase, "the created co-creator."[11]

PROPER 13

Psalm 145:8-9, 15-22 is the RCL Psalm. See the commentary for Proper 13 B, where this is discussed in connection with the Johannine account of the feeding of the 5,000.

Psalm 104:25-31 is the LBW Psalm for 11 Pentecost.

See the discussion of this text for Pentecost. Here, in view of the day's gospel, God's provision of food for all creatures (vv. 28-29) might be stressed. God is always doing, in ways to which we have become accustomed, what Jesus does so dramatically. The Spirit, "the LORD and giver of life" in the Nicene Creed, is involved in a fundamental way in the sustenance of life (v. 31).

Matthew 14:13-21 (LBW for 11 Pentecost.)

Some preachers are a bit embarrassed when they have to treat miracle stories for a congregation familiar with the scientific understanding of the world. But it is hard to avoid these stories in the gospels, so it is a good idea to think about how they may be proclaimed without either a fundamentalist defiance of science or elimination from the narratives of all references to events in the physical world.

There are various approaches which can be taken to miracles like the feeding of the 5,000 in the present text. One may argue that the miracle account does not refer to events which "really happened" in a physical sense, but is a story intended to make a theological point. If that were true, we would not have to face the question of natural laws. But we have to consider the likelihood that at least some of the miracle stories of the Bible do refer to things which "really happened." Jesus certainly had a reputation as a miracle worker, and it is unlikely that this would have developed if nothing marvelous had ever happened in his presence.

At one end of the spectrum of realistic interpretations, one may argue that God simply did break into the network of casual relations which the ordinary laws of nature describe. Natural laws only describe the general behavior of the world, and a claim that isolated events in conflict with those laws have happened is not disproved by the much greater number of observations which support those laws. This would agree with the popular view — which is a relatively late development in Christian thought[12] — of miracles as "violations" of the laws of nature.

At the other end of the spectrum is the view of miracle stories as accounts of things which took place in accord with known laws of science, but which have been told and perhaps embellished to emphasize some theological theme. An example of such interpretation in the present case is the "social miracle" theory. According to this, Jesus got some people (the disciples in the synoptics or the boy of John 6:9) to share their lunches with others. This example of generosity moved others to share the food that *they* had brought along, so that all were fed.

There is another way of thinking about the matter, in a way intermediate between these two. This is the idea that God, in the beginning, created the world so that miraculous events could unfold in accord with a rational pattern (though perhaps one differing at critical points from the laws that we know) and with God's will in order to produce unusual phenomena like a sudden multiplication of food. There is a suggestion of this idea in the Jewish tradition in *Pirke Aboth*, where there is a list of things which God created on the evening of the sixth day.[13] This includes Aaron's rod which budded miraculously and, significantly for our present text, the manna. Thus God would have built a "natural" possibility for what we now see as miraculous events into the world through the divine acts of creation in the beginning.

There is an underlying point even more basic than the question of which of these approaches we should follow. C.S. Lewis pointed out that, in stories like the feeding of the 5,000, Jesus is doing, in a sudden and sharply focussed way, what God is doing all the time through natural processes.[14] (See the comments on the Psalms suggested for this day, 104 or 145.) In nature, a little grain grows into a lot of grain through cell division, photosynthesis, and other processes describable by science. In today's gospel, a little grain again becomes a lot of grain, and similarly for the fish. *How* this is done is not explained, but the point is that the miracle is a *sign* (note John's consistent use of this word *semeion*) that the creator is present in Jesus. As Lewis notes, Jesus turns down the suggestion (Matthew 4:3-4) that he turn stones into bread. It isn't done that way!

This miracle story shows Jesus as the One who has power to feed, to preserve life, in an extraordinary way. He is no mere mortal. Yet he calls his disciples to share in his vocation. "You give them something to eat." Jesus' followers must take upon themselves the responsibility of being partners in his work.

All our scientific knowledge and technological ability may seem like only "five loaves and two fish" when we look out on the world and see how far the little we have must reach. Our ability to preserve health and heal would have been considered miraculous by earlier generations, yet we send home the multitudes who are aged or jobless if they have no health insurance. Our agricultural technology is staggering, but millions starve or are undernourished. Our gross national product is immense, but many are born and die homeless. Where will we find clean water and productive soil to feed a rapidly expanding world population?

Jesus said, "They need not go away; you give them something to eat." Habitat for Humanity and other housing providers are springing up everywhere. Global mission boards sponsor agricultural stations, fish-farming projects, and other technological resources to feed the multitudes. What other things can faithful Christians do?

PROPER 16

Romans 12:1-8 (LBW for 15 Pentecost.)

One of the biblical images which is quite useful for the science-theology dialogue is that of the Church as the Body of Christ. Teilhard de Chardin suggested that the Body of Christ is the next stage in evolution. The present passage is a brief but important presentation of this image. In particular, the abilities given to some Christians for work in scientific and technological fields should be seen as spiritual gifts intended for the growth of the Body. (Exodus 31:1-11 is of interest here. See our discussion of it in the Free Text section.)

PROPER 19

Exodus 15:1b-11 is given as an alternative by RCL. For discussion see Easter C.

PROPER 22

Philippians 3:12-21 is LBW's Second Lesson for 20 Pentecost. See the commentary for 2 Lent C for discussion of vv. 20-21.

Psalm 19 is given as an alternative by RCL. For discussion see 3 Lent B.

PROPER 23

Isaiah 25:1-9 (LBW has vv. 6-9 for 21 Pentecost.)

Israel did not from its beginnings have an idea of bodily resurrection. That appears only in late parts of the Old Testament with an apocalyptic bent, such as the present text and Daniel 12. The physical imagery here is very vivid, showing the value which the material world had for the Hebrews. Death really can be "swallowed up" forever if somehow the material world described by science shares in the victory which God wins over the powers of destruction.

PROPER 24

Psalm 96 (LBW for 22 Pentecost.)

This Psalm celebrates God's kingship over the world. All people are to rejoice in that rule — but also the heavens, the seas, and "all the trees of the wood." That ought to make some difference for our decisions about the environment: our dumping of wastes in the oceans or clearing of forests will affect the choir which sings before God's throne.

Of course the trees can't *really* sing. It is only (of organisms which we've so far encountered) human beings who can voice their *conscious* praises. Consequently, we have the responsibility to voice the praises of other creatures on their behalf, and it makes no sense to do that unless we accept the responsibility to *care* for the rest of creation too.

While it is important to call Christians to practical work to protect the environment, this text gives an opportunity to remind congregations that our environmental involvement is to have a *doxological* element as well. The praise and thanks which we sing in church are the voice of the "choir," leading the praise of God by the whole "congregation" of creation. And, in turn, a doxological criterion can be applied to anything we do which affects the environment. We should ask about any of our activities, "Does this contribute to the praise of God?"

(Early Christian apologists argued that the full reading of v. 10 was "the LORD has reigned *from the wood*": a marginal note inspired by "wood" in v. 12 may have crept into the text. That is the origin of the third verse of the hymn "The Royal Banners Forward Go." The true worship of God is centered on the cross.)

Matthew 22:15-22 (LBW for 22 Pentecost.)

Which things belong to the rulers of this world and which to God? The question is posed by this text, but is not answered. When considering a specific problem of how to deploy scientific knowledge, technological capacity, and natural or human resources, does Caesar have authority? How is ultimate authority brought to bear within human history?

In the conflict between using for healing a new drug which may be an abortifacient, what obedience do we render to the emperor who makes the rules for a particular people? When one nation allows the use of marijuana to treat cancer patients and another will not, what obedience is due to the emperor? What determines responsible medical practice? Whose authority governs ocean waters in which trawling for tuna threatens other large sea life? What international authority can prevent the Amazon rain forests from being levelled, and if there is none, can a "divine imperative" be invoked effectively to protect the planet?

On what basis do we determine the form of our obedience to God in any of these situations? Jesus answered the question in his situation by going to the cross. Is there a way of the cross for scientists, technologists, medical practitioners, or conservationists? How does the Church present its challenge today as part of faithful proclamation of the gospel? What are the limits of cross-bearing as a reason for civil disobedience? If you pay the price, does that justify such disobedience? How do we determine when it is appropriate to say with Luther, "Here I stand. God help me, I cannot do otherwise"?

PROPER 25

Psalm 90:1-6, 13-17 is given as an alternative by RCL. For discussion see Proper 28 A.

PROPER 27

Amos 5:18-24 (LBW for 24 Pentecost.)

"Let justice roll down like waters, and righteousness like an everflowing stream" (v. 24). This verse has usually been applied to justice issues as they affect people living in the present. Scientific and technological stewardship of the earth and its resources calls us to think of future generations, and of the nonhuman creation as well, when we respond to Amos' call.

A comparatively few people around the world become rich as present natural resources are used or polluted. Where can the Church use its voice as an advocate for future generations as well as for today's oppressed, refugees, or hungry? What bills designed to protect resources are now before the legislature? How can future generations be educated to ensure a concern for the larger issues of justice? How can the Church have an impact on the education and formation of individuals by the state?

Amos, concerned about justice for all the people of Israel, challenges preachers to look at the world of their generation and raise for people of their day the issues he raised in the eighth century B.C. Materials from church agencies and expertise from within each congregation can be resources for pastors as they interpret Amos for today.

PROPER 28

Psalm 90 (RCL has vv. 1-8 [9-11] 12, while LBW has vv. 12-17 for 25 Pentecost.)

This somber Psalm reminds us of our mortality, and "the work of our hands" shares in that mortality. It is true that with our scientific understanding of the world and science-based technology we have passed beyond simply being able to rearrange the things which occur in nature. Computers and transgenic species represent qualitative changes in the world. Still, they are "the work of our hands," and we should look to God to prosper them. Only if such works are accomplished in genuine wisdom can they be counted part of "the glory and honor of the nations" which finally will be brought into the City of God (Revelation 21:26).

Zephaniah 1:7, 12-18 (This text is not used in LBW.)

If Psalm 90 produces a somber mood, we may be brought into a state of absolute dread by Zephaniah's prophecy of doom. (It is the basis of the medieval hymn *Dies Irae,* known to many from the film *Amadeus.*) What are we to make of "the great day of the LORD" which will be a day "of wrath, a day of distress and anguish," and so forth (vv. 14-15)? Especially if we are considering the role of technology in our lives, how should we react to the prophet who cries out that,

> *Their wealth shall be plundered,*
> *and their houses laid waste.*

> *Though they build houses,*
> *they shall not inhabit them;*
> *Though they plant vineyards,*
> *they shall not drink wine from them* (v. 13)?

In the prophetic tradition, the technological activities of *building* and *planting* were metaphors for the human vocation. (See, for example, Isaiah 65:21; Jeremiah 1:10, 31:28, 35:7; Ezekiel 28:26; and Amos 9:14. In the commentary for 4 Epiphany C we discuss this more fully.) The prophet uses this image to describe the ultimate plight of those who sin against the Lord.

Zephaniah reiterates the prophetic theme that no human technology, not fortified cities or lofty battlements (v. 16), can stand against God's righteous wrath. He speaks out against our attempts to ignore God's place in the scheme of things and decries the perennial error of using technology to "make a name for ourselves" (Genesis 11:4 — see the commentary for Pentecost C).

In preaching this text we must realize that it represents one side of the prophetic vision of God's response to human sin. That vision is not of judgment alone, but also of redemption and renewal. (See the commentary for 4 Epiphany C.) We can use this prophecy of doom to explore how our technologically-ordered world embodies human sin. With the metaphor of building and planting we can then also preach hope for renewal and the possibility of developing technology appropriate to the will of God. (For a discussion of "appropriate technology" see the commentary for 1 Advent A.)

CHRIST THE KING

Ezekiel 34:11-16, 20-24 (LBW has vv. 11-16, 23-24.)

This passage about God's bringing Israel back from exile does not have obvious scientific or technological themes.

However, verse 12 in particular suggests some attention to a concern which space travel may bring: How will God deal with human beings who have been scattered by interplanetary or interstellar migration? An example of a story sermon addressing this question is given in Appendix E.

DAY OF THANKSGIVING

Psalm 65 (See the discussion for Harvest in the section of Common Texts.)

Deuteronomy 8:1-18 (RCL has vv. 7-18, while LBW gives vv. 1-10.)

Verses 7-10 call Israel's attention to the physical blessings of the land which God gives it. As we often emphasize, these blessings — the fertility of the ground, its water and its minerals — come about through natural processes. It will be difficult for people to thank God for such things if they think that they are to be attributed simply to "nature," and that God really has nothing to do with them. For that reason, it may be a good idea to place some emphasis on doctrines of creation and providence, and the concept that God works through the processes of nature, for Thanksgiving.

Endnotes

1. Some commentators consider this oracle to be part of Second Isaiah. See, e.g., John L. McKenzie, *Second Isaiah,* The Anchor Bible 20 (Doubleday, Garden City NY, 1968), pp. 9-12.

2. Pierre Teilhard de Chardin, *Hymn of the Universe* (Harper & Row, New York, 1965).

3. Aloys Grillmeier, *Christ in Christian Tradition,* 2nd ed. (John Knox, Atlanta, 1975), pp. 321 and 531.

4. George L. Murphy, *The Trademark Of God* (Morehouse-Barlow, Wilton CT, 1986).

5. Banesh Hoffmann, *The Strange Story of the Quantum,* 2nd ed. (Dover, New York, 1959), p. 232.

6. Ernest C. Messenger, *Evolution and Theology* (Macmillan, New York, 1932).

7. Lynn White, Jr., "The Historical Roots of our Ecological Crisis," *Science 155*, 1967, 1203.

8. Ronald Cole-Turner, *The New Genesis: Theology and the Genetic Revolution* (Westminster/John Knox, Louisville KY, 1993).

9. Karl Barth, *Christ and Adam* (Harper & Brothers, New York, 1957).

10. Friedrich Dürrenmatt, *The Physicists* (Grove, New York, 1983), pp. 93-94.

11. Philip Hefner, *The Human Factor* (Fortress, Minneapolis, 1993), especially Chapter 2.

12. Christopher Kaiser, *Creation and the History of Science* (Wm. B. Eerdmans, Grand Rapids MI, 1991), pp. 30-33.

13. R. Travers Herford, *The Ethics of the Talmud: Sayings of the Fathers* (Schocken, New York, 1962), pp. 129-131.

14. C.S. Lewis, *Miracles* (Macmillan, New York, 1947), especially pp. 141-142.

Year B

1 ADVENT

Mark 13:24-37 (LBW has Mark 13:33-37 as one option. Our comments refer to vv. 24-27.)

The apocalyptic imagery of such texts contrasts sharply with the scientific picture of the world. Given our knowledge of the distances, sizes, and compositions of the stars, what could it *mean* to talk about the stars of heaven literally falling (v. 25)? That alone may convince us that such a text cannot be read as a detailed scenario of the way that the physical universe will come to an end.

And yet — the fact that the celestial powers, as well as the physical structure of the earth and political, religious, and social events are involved here makes us realize that what Jesus, other Jews of his time, and the early church had in mind when they thought of the future was something which encompassed the whole universe. If we are to be faithful to the biblical witness, we will have to take seriously the cosmic character of its eschatology. We must be willing to stretch our theological and scientific thinking to do it justice, even as we resist the temptation to constrain our eschatology within the limits of the physical cosmology of the first century.

2 ADVENT

Isaiah 40:1-11

There are many ways to reflect on these opening verses of Second Isaiah in the Advent season. Here we may simply note the connection with the day's Second Lesson in the contrast between the ephemeral character of earthly life and the permanence of God's word.

2 Peter 3:8-15a (LBW ends with v. 14.)

In what is perhaps the latest writing of the canon there is still a looking forward to the dramatic consummation of all things. The elements (*stoicheia,* from which the branch of chemistry called stoichiometry gets its name) will be "burned up with fervent heat" (KJV). But even with this destructive imagery there is a positive note of hope for "new heavens and a new earth."

The early verses (and one should really go back to the beginning of the chapter to get the whole train of thought) show a clear awareness of the problem of "the delay of the parousia" which has vexed Christianity in one way or another since the first century. The author of 2 Peter argues (see also Psalm 90:4) that God's time scale is quite different from ours. Thirty human generations amount only to a day for God.

A simple illustration can help people to put the matter in perspective. It took between ten and fifteen billion years for human life to emerge after the big bang. If ten billion years were compressed into a single year, the period of two thousand years which has elapsed since the time of Jesus would be about six seconds. On a cosmic scale, the resurrection of Jesus took place just yesterday. Seen in that light, there does not seem to have been any real delay of the parousia at all!

3 ADVENT

Isaiah 61:1-4, 8-11 (LBW has vv. 1-4, 10-11.)

Building upon ancient ruins and former devastations in biblical times usually had to do with the need to rebuild after the ravages of war. The days are upon us, however, when we need to say the same for reclaiming deserts, cleaning up rivers, oceans and lakes, replenishing forests, and repairing damage to the ozone layer. God's people are to minister to those involved in such work, encouraging understandings that make such renewal possible.

Isaiah's vision appears to be that of a people who, as priests and ministers in a society being redeemed, will be the apex of that society, the wealthy who control and lead with the vision which they hold before the people. If we see this together with Jesus' vision of a servant ministry then we have a picture of servant rulers, of woman and man created and set in the garden to take care of it and to rule over it by cultivating it in the best possible way under God's authority.

4 ADVENT

Psalm 89:1-4, 19-26 (LBW has vv. 1-4, 14-18.)

It's a shame to have to take just pieces of this Psalm which expresses praise to God as creator (1-8), remembrance of the Davidic covenant (19-37), and lament for the king's present misfortune (38-51), with a doxological conclusion to the third book of the psalter. The whole is a great expression of the psalms as the prayers of Christ. The second section connects well with the First Lesson and Gospel. Verses 9 and 10 use the image of the primordial battle with chaos for God's creative work, a victory over the powers which oppose the ordering of the cosmos. This can be connected in one direction with God's establishment of the order displayed in the laws of nature (cf. Isaiah 45:18), and in another with the *Christus Victor* motif for speaking about salvation.

1 CHRISTMAS

Psalm 148 is discussed for this Sunday in Year A.

Psalm 111 is assigned for this Sunday each year by LBW. We treat it for 4 Epiphany B.

Luke 2:22-40 (LBW has vv. 25-40.)

In the Evangelical Lutheran Church in America this last Sunday of the calendar year is noted as "Student Recognition Sunday." (A lot of college students will be home for the holidays.) The note at the end of the gospel that the child Jesus "grew ... filled with wisdom" would be a fitting note for such a day. It is important for churches to recognize and encourage in particular their students who are pursuing work in science and technology. It is easy to point out the benefits and threats which can come from such work. Science and technology cannot generate their own ethical imperatives for the use of their knowledge and techniques. Ethics requires a more profound basis, and Christianity offers the category of "wisdom," the wisdom whose beginning is the fear of the Lord. (See the final verse of Psalm 111 and our discussions for 5 Epiphany A and Proper 18 C.)

2 EPIPHANY

Psalm 139:1-17 (We have included vv. 6-11.)

This is one of the classic statements of God's omnipresence. As vv. 12-17 especially make clear, this is more than a matter of God's passively "being there." God is actively present, working in all the hidden processes of nature, such as the complex and subtle activities of embryological development and human growth.

These take place through processes, explainable in principle by scientific laws, and also through the creative and providential operations of God. It is not an either/or matter, but one of God's being involved in the whole of nature. This is the thrust of what was described in traditional doctrines of providence as "concurrence" or "co-operation": God works *with* natural processes, so that things happen "naturally" *and* through God's action. With this idea there is no need to think that God is eliminated by the discovery of scientific explanations for phenomena *or* that God is necessary as an element of scientific explanation.

Psalm 67 is appointed by LBW for this Sunday. See the commentary for Proper 15 A.

John 1:43-51 is given as an alternative by RCL. For discussion see Saint Bartholomew's Day in the section of texts common to each year.

4 EPIPHANY

Psalm 111 (LBW has a different Psalm.)

Over the great door of the Cavendish Laboratory at Cambridge University is the inscription

*Magna opera Domini
exquisitia in omnes voluptates eius.*[1]

This is the Latin of the second verse of today's Psalm,

"Great are the deeds of the LORD!
They are studied by all who delight in them."

The psalmist had in mind both God's historical acts on behalf of Israel (vv. 6, 9) and God's provisions for people's needs in creation (v. 5). The great Cambridge scientists like James Clerk Maxwell saw God's works also in the natural processes of mechanics, thermodynamics, and electromagnetism which could be described by precise mathematical laws like Maxwell's equations for the electromagnetic field. (For those equations see the commentary on 2 Corinthians 4:5-12 for Proper 4 B.) "The deeds of the LORD" include all of those things, as well as God's acts in salvation history.

Many Christians have been led to think that there must be "warfare" between faith and science, and they may have the uneasy feeling that science is always making Christianity more and more irrelevant. A person certainly does not need to be a Christian (or, indeed, to have any explicit religious faith) in order to be a great scientist, but there is also no need for conflict between scientific work and religious belief. It may be helpful for preachers to call attention to scientists like Maxwell (who is outranked perhaps only by Newton and Einstein on the honor roll of great physicists) who have been committed Christians. "Men of science," he said, "as well as other men need to learn from Christ."[2]

5 EPIPHANY

Mark 1:29-39

Healing was a major part of Jesus' ministry, and the Book of Acts tells us that continued in the early Church. How are we to think of such work today?

Some of the general discussion of miracles for Proper 13 A is applicable here. In the case of healings, we know that the mind can have a very strong influence on the body. There are many healings which are in this way "natural," even though we don't understand their mechanism. Many cures in response to prayer, "faith healers," and apparent miracles by non-Christians (e.g., those recorded of the Emperor Vespasian by Suetonius) may fall in this category. Some of Jesus' healings as well can be understood in this way, with no need to appeal to "violations of the laws of nature."

And yet we ought not use "psychosomatic" as a magic word to avoid further questions about such cures. Many of the people Jesus is said to have cured (e.g., Mark 5:25; 9:21; John 5:5) had been sick for a long time. If health were just a matter of wanting to be well, they wouldn't have needed Jesus. We may see Jesus not only as the one who heals by means of a person's faith but as the one who through the

Spirit creates such faith. (Paul describes saving faith in Christ as something only the Holy Spirit can give in 1 Corinthians 12:3.) These surprising healings may be natural, but they cluster about Jesus in a remarkable way.

A point to be noted especially in Mark is the association of illness with demonic powers, and thus of healing with exorcism. Bacteria and viruses are creatures of God, but Jesus shows God's opposition to the destruction which such agents work in human lives. The classical Christian view sees demons as fallen angelic powers which were originally created good by God, and which remain in essence good.[3] It may be difficult in a scientific world to see a relationship between traditional views of the demonic and disease, but some of the fundamental themes can be appropriately demythologized.

7 EPIPHANY

Isaiah 43:18-25

God promises to renew the desert to provide water for the wild beasts and birds who will honor God and for the people whom God has chosen. Divine power is established over nature as well as over a covenant people.

God has given people power to renew the desert through irrigation techniques and ways of caring for the soil that remove impurities and make rich farmland. In Israel, one of us spoke with a man whose parents had come from the Soviet Union in the 1920s. They received a desert-like parcel of land laden with salts and small stones which made it difficult to farm. He said that each year his father would go over the land on his knees, running the dirt through a sifter inch by inch to take away larger impure parts and leave more fertile soil. Each year he would raise what crops he could, and then sift it again to remove unproductive material which had worked its way to the surface.

For twenty years he did this until he had a plot of rich soil. And each year he would show his son the harvest and say, "God has given us this good land as our gift." So, too, each of us must work faithfully where God has called us, using the knowledge God has given. At harvest time we are to remember that God has given us the land and brings about its fruitfulness.

8 EPIPHANY

Hosea 2:14-20 (LBW's suggestion that vv. 17-18 be omitted should be ignored, as should most suggested excisions.)

The prophet reminds Israel, and us, that God's covenant is not just with one group of people, or even with all humanity. The Noachic covenant (Genesis 9:8-17) is between God and "every living creature," and Hosea promises the renewal of that pledge by God.

The theme of God's covenant with nature is important in today's climate of concern about the environment. Nature is more than a backdrop or a support system for the human race. It is valuable enough to God in its own right that God "negotiates" a covenant which includes nature as well as humankind. Humanity is included in the agreement and comes in for special consideration, in part because of its destructive propensities (v. 18).

The special role of the wilderness should be noted here. The prophet speaks of a future recapitulation of Israel's history in which the people will be brought back into the wilderness where they began. God will give Israel the higher agricultural technology of Canaanite culture, but in a way which will not allow that culture to seduce Israel (Hosea 2:5-13). In the wilderness, where reliance on God is an everyday necessity, Israel will come to know its Lord as the one who gives them the blessings of agriculture.

TRANSFIGURATION

2 Corinthians 4:3-6 (See the discussion for Proper 4 B.)

1 LENT

Genesis 9:8-17 (LBW has a different First Lesson.)

This is the only Sunday for which part of the Flood story is used. (Selections from it are the second reading for the Easter Vigil.) One point to emphasize is that God's covenant is not only with all people but even with "every living creature that is with you." This covenant, which is renewed in Jesus' death and resurrection, shows God's intention to sustain and to save all creation. Awareness of the scope of the covenant should provide a powerful basis for the care of the earth.

Mark 1:9-15 (LBW has vv. 12-15.)

In our discussion of Matthew's temptation story for 1 Lent A we noted the theme of *recapitulation.* (See also the preceding comments for 8 Epiphany. This idea is strong in Hosea.) There it was Israel's experience in the wilderness which was replayed by Jesus, who did not succumb to the temptations which defeated the ancestors. That note is missing in Mark's briefer account.

But the mention of "wild beasts" with Jesus in the wilderness may carry us back even further, to the first human in Eden with the beasts (Genesis 2:18-20). This earth creature, the *'adham,* named the animals, also formed from the ground, as their fellow creature who yet had special gifts to care for them. Only the "one flesh," man and woman, could be full partners. But though they had distinctive gifts which set them apart from the other animals, they did not resist the temptation to have *more* than that, to be "like God" (Genesis 3:5). Jesus, however, who *has* the "form of God," does not yield to the temptation to cling to it (Philippians 2:5-11), and thus succeeds where humanity failed before.

Mark's statement that Jesus was simply "with" the wild animals suggests a lack of hostility, an absence of fear on the animals' part and of exploitation on the part of the new Adam. The great Ruthwell Cross (c. A.D. 700) in southern Scotland has one panel showing Jesus standing over two pig-like animals, with a Latin inscription which may be translated, "Jesus Christ, the righteous judge. Beasts and dragons knew in the desert the savior of the world."

The theme of recapitulations has been influential in evolutionary biology, a point of some importance for theology. Each of us carries reminders of our relationships with other animals — the structures of bones and muscles and the chemical makeup of DNA and proteins. The embryological development of human beings has similarities with those of other mammals, so that at early stages it is hard to distinguish a human embryo from that of a dog or monkey. Haeckel's idea in the nineteenth century that the embryo goes through the evolutionary history in an accelerated way ("ontogeny recapitulates phylogeny") was a vast and inaccurate oversimplification. Still, embryological relationships between humans and other species do exist.

And those relationships are shared by Jesus as well. Fully human, he participates in the history of the human race, and is thus organically related to the "wild beasts." And because the beasts are thus related to God Incarnate, they share in the hope of salvation which he brings. C.S. Lewis seems to have been the first to see the connection between the biological and the theological themes of recapitulation.

He comes down; down from the heights of absolute being into time and space, down into humanity; down

> *further still, if embryologists are right, to recapitulate in the womb ancient and pre-human phases of life; down to the very roots and sea-bed of the Nature He had created. But He goes down to come up again and bring the whole ruined world up with Him.*[4]

It will be surprising, and at first disturbing, for some Christians to hear such language. But it should also be comforting. God's willingness to share in our pre-human ancestry shows the depth to which God is willing to go in order to save us.

A preacher who wants to address this topic should resist the temptation simply to give a lecture. One way of presenting the idea of God's recapitulation of history in a sermon would be to develop a science fiction story with a time travel theme. (Time travel has been a common plot device of science fiction writers, but has also received some serious scientific attention recently.[5]) An example of such a story sermon motivated by the present text is given in Appendix E.

2 LENT

Psalm 115:1, 9-18 is given by LBW for this Sunday. But vv. 2-8 should not be omitted, especially in Lent.

Nobody worships Chemosh or Marduk anymore, so idols of gold and silver (v. 4) may seem irrelevant. But modern technological society has its own gods of metal. We can hardly avoid them, going from the toaster in the morning, in the car to get to work with the computer, and finishing up in the evening with the television. Not that technology is intrinsically evil — far from it! It represents the goodness of creation and our role as created co-creators if used for the right purposes and used as means rather than ends. Idolatry is always a matter of exalting something which is intrinsically good to a place above God, the place of ultimate reliance.

That can be a problem especially with military technology, for there is a great temptation to depend on weapons systems for ultimate security. Christians may think of militarism as a problem involving destruction and death, but may need help in seeing it as a First Commandment problem. In Shakespeare's *Henry V*, after the Battle of Agincourt, the King says, "Do we all holy rites: Let there be sung *Non nobis* and *Te Deum."* *Non Nobis* is the Latin title of Psalm 115, "Not to us." In Branagh's recent film of *Henry V* there is a beautiful singing of the first verse of the Psalm as the soldiers struggle across the muddy and gory battlefield, walking past corpses and supporting the wounded. This is not a cynical or simplistic put-down of war; Shakespeare and most of the Christian tradition have recognized the legitimacy of war under some circumstances. But there is an awareness of the realities of war, and of whom our reliance is to be in peace or in war. "Not to us, O LORD, not to us, but to your name give glory."

Verse 16 corresponds to the delegation to humanity of "dominion over the earth" in Genesis 1. Humanity is to care for the earth as God's representative, in the image and likeness of God. That may be seen in light of the fact that this Psalm, according to Jewish custom for Passover, would have been part of the "hymn" which Jesus and his disciples sang before going out to the Mount of Olives "in the night in which he was betrayed" (Mark 14:26). Sacrificial self-giving is the model of rule which God Incarnate sets before us.

3 LENT

Psalm 19 (LBW has vv. 8-14, which speak of God's revelation in Torah, a connection with the First Lesson. Understanding is deepened if the earlier verses, which speak of nature's witness to God, are also read. It is no accident that they are parts of the same Psalm!)

Faithful Jews and Christians, together with many people who simply "believe in God," agree that "the heavens declare the glory of God." But others, including some famous scientists, will respond, "Not to me!" It is not lack of *intelligence* which leads some scientists to deny any sign of divine activity in the cosmos. Has something gone wrong with the psalmist's argument?

After speaking of the glory of God in nature, the Psalm turns to the Torah, God's gift of the Law to Israel. It is that which "revives," "gives wisdom," "rejoices the heart," and "gives light" — things which are *not* said of nature. Through God's revelation in Torah one is able to know who God is, and then to recognize this God of Israel as the One whose glory the heavens declare. There is a revelation in nature and a proper natural theology, but any *independent* natural theology is ruled out by the fact that Torah is necessary for enlightenment. A proper natural theology must thus be seen as part of the religion of Israel, not an independent prologue to it — let alone as something which can take the place of Torah.

The same idea follows through into Christian thought. We see the true God's activity in the universe only when we begin with the belief that God is the One revealed in Jesus, to whom the Law bears witness. The God whose handiwork is shown in the universe is the Crucified.

The second half of Psalm 19 may have been added to the first as a conscious corrective to the idea of an independent natural theology. If so, there was a clear sense within the canonical process that natural theology is by itself inadequate.

John 2:13-22

The "dwelling" of God is a theme which runs throughout the Bible. We read of God's travels with Abraham, Isaac, and Israel, the Ark and the tabernacle, and all the attention given to the temples in Jerusalem. The Hebrew canon, which begins with God's creation of heaven and earth in Genesis 1, ends with the command to "build a house" for "the God of heaven" (2 Chronicles 36:23). In view of that, the presence of God's Spirit in Genesis 1:2 can be seen as a consecration of the universe to be God's dwelling. The universe is created as a suitable site for the development of life, and thus for the Incarnation.

In the infancy narratives of Matthew and Luke, the Holy Spirit comes upon Mary, so that the child born of her is consecrated as God's unique dwelling. In our text from John 2, Jesus takes the place of the Temple as the place where God "tabernacles" with us (cf. John 1:14). This all looks forward to the end of the *Greek* Scriptures, where "the dwelling of God is with humanity" (Revelation 21:3)[6], and the temple in the heavenly city come to earth is "the Lord God the Almighty and the Lamb" (Revelation 21:22).

Psalm 111 is given as an alternative by RCL. For discussion see Epiphany B.

5 LENT

John 12:20-33

"I, when I am lifted up from the earth, will draw all people to myself," Jesus says in v. 32. The modern image which comes to mind here is that of the cross as a *magnet,* creating a force field which draws men and women to it. The "moral influence" theory of the atonement in particular can be described vividly as a "magnet model,"[7] though the use of such imagery need not be limited to that particular view of the work of Christ. This is not just a sermon illustration to be *talked* about. A magnet could be used, perhaps in a children's sermon, in order to illustrate Jesus' words about the cross.

Some manuscripts have here *panta,* "all things," rather than *pantas,* "all people." This would present the Crucified as the One who reconciles the entire universe to God, as in Colossians 1:20.

EASTER DAY

Isaiah 25:6-9 is one RCL suggestion for this festival. See the commentary for Proper 23 A.

2 EASTER

Psalm 148 is appointed by LBW for this Sunday. See the commentary for 1 Christmas A.

3 EASTER

Psalm 139:1-11 is appointed by LBW for this Sunday. See the discussion for 2 Epiphany B.

6 EASTER

Psalm 98

Like Psalm 148 (1 Christmas), this is a praise of God by the entire world, but the theme is not as fully developed here.

PENTECOST

Psalm 104:25-35, 37 (See commentary for Pentecost A.)

Romans 8:22-27 is one RCL option for the Second Lesson. See the discussion for Proper 11 A.

PROPER 4

2 Corinthians 4:5-12 (LBW for 2 Pentecost.)

A number of years ago the American Institute of Physics put out a button with the following inscription:

"And God said:
$$\nabla \cdot \mathbf{D} = 4\pi\rho$$
$$\nabla \cdot \mathbf{B} = 0$$
$$\nabla \times \mathbf{H} = (4\pi/c)\,\mathbf{J} + (1/c)\,\partial \mathbf{D}/\partial t$$
$$\nabla \times \mathbf{E} = -(1/c)\,\partial \mathbf{B}/\partial t$$
and there was light."

(T-shirts are also available with this inscription.)

The famous Maxwell equations of electromagnetic theory do show how light can be described as electromagnetic waves. Our understanding of Genesis 1:3 must somehow involve God's thinking and choosing a part of the world's pattern which can be described approximately with these equations. (It is worth noting that Maxwell, to whom we are indebted for these equations and many other scientific discoveries, was a committed Christian as well as being one of the greatest of physicists.) Paul's use of the Genesis story warns us, however, against a deistic picture of God's writing down a set of equations at the beginning and then simply letting the universe run in accord with those rules. God is profoundly involved with the world, and the image of the creation of light can also be used to describe God's revelation in Christ.

Jesus' resurrection is like the creation of light on the first day, except that it is here no created light which illumines us but the light which is God's own self-expression (John 1:4-9). It is, as some Christian mystics have said, "the uncreated light of Tabor."

Psalm 139:1-6, 13-18 is given as an alternative by RCL. For discussion see 3 Easter B.

Psalm 96 is given as an alternative by RCL. For discussion see Proper 24 A.

PROPER 5

Genesis 3:8-15 (LBW has vv. 9-15 for 3 Pentecost.)

The familiar story of the Fall continues the stories of creation and thus the story of the emergence of the human vocation. Verses 17-19 imply that the work of "tilling and keeping" are now involved, along with the rest of human life, with sin.

The technological ordering of our lives, though not in itself evil, provides occasion for human sin. For instance, the extent of pollution in our time is due, at least in part, to greed and shortsightedness. Technology itself is not condemned any more than humanity itself. But our use of technology displays human sin, as does any other form of human activity today.

PROPER 6

Psalm 20 is given as an alternative by RCL. For discussion see National Holiday in the section of texts common to each year.

PROPER 7

Job 38:1-11; Psalm 107:1-3, 23-32; Mark 4:35-41 (LBW for 5 Pentecost. LBW also has 2 Corinthians 5:14-21 as the Second Lesson, whereas RCL has vv. 14-17 for the previous Sunday.)

These fit together in a way that the readings for a given Sunday seldom do. God speaks to Job out of the whirlwind and sets out the wonders of creation. The psalmist speaks of God's deliverance from the power of the sea, and in the Gospel it is Jesus who saves from a storm on the water. With that connection in mind, it is no wonder that the disciples exclaim, "Who then is this, that even the wind and the sea obey him?" Since the Creator is personally present in Jesus, Paul says that "anyone who is in Christ is a new creation." All the readings focus on creation and new creation, with the sea as a symbol of the primordial chaos which God restrained in the beginning (Job 38:8), and from which God still protects the cosmos.

Our science has made us even more aware of the scope of creation, of distant galaxies and black holes, and raises new scientific questions. And with all those questions, we affirm that the God in whom we trust is able to comprehend all of creation, and indeed is its author.

As we marvel at God's power to open the universe infinitely, we, like Job, humbly bow our hearts in faith that surely this God also has the power to open up the future for us and to create new possibilities in our lives. New opportunities and joys which all our science and philosophy may not have dreamed of may lie before us. Some of those opportunities may lie in the realm of God-given abilities to develop protections against storms and other natural disasters, possibilities no one imagined a few centuries ago.

2 Corinthians 6:1-11 is RCL's Second Lesson. See the discussion for Ash Wednesday.

PROPER 8

Mark 5:21-43 (LBW has 5:21-24a, 35-43 *or* 24b-34. We focus on the later verses here.)

The woman in the story had "endured much under many physicians" for twelve years. That does not reflect very well on the medical profession. It is perhaps significant that Luke omits the statement (but Matthew does as well).

Physicians today are vastly more skilled than those of biblical times, but people still may suffer under them, and under systems of medical care, perhaps even while their physical ailments are being cured. No matter how scientific and successful medical science becomes, it is still important for patients to be treated as persons, not just as machinery to be maintained or repaired.

PROPER 9

Mark 6:1-13 (LBW has vv. 7-13 for 8 Pentecost.)

As part of their missionary activity, Jesus' disciples "anointed with oil many who were sick and cured them." This practice was carried on by the early Church (cf. James 5:13-15), and developed into a rite of anointing of the sick. It has been seen (when the emphasis has not been primarily on preparation for death) as a particularly religious means of healing.

The oil that the disciples used, however, would have been seen by them and by the sick they treated as a common medicine. (For medicinal use of olive oil see, e.g., Isaiah 1:6 and Luke 10:34.) The religious use of this medicine consisted in prayer and faith that God would heal through it.

Today we have medicines which are, physically, far more effective than olive oil. But it may be understood as a symbolic medicine. When we pray for healing, it is not for us to tell God *how* to heal. Our everyday experience, however, tells us that the vast majority of cures take place by natural processes available through medicine, surgery, diet, radiation, and so forth. A rite of anointing is a way of asking for God's blessings through those means and of strengthening faith that God heals by them.

Religious approaches to healing parallel, and do not supplant, medical means. The old "Exhortation" when "The Patient Prays on Taking Medicine" in Stark's 1720 *Prayer Hand-Book* remains an excellent statement of this. After quoting the passage from James, it says:

> *If a devout prayer is indispensable even in times of health, how can a patient neglect it, particularly when he takes medicine?*
>
> *1. The patient must not despise the physician, nor his medicine, nor think that if he is destined to recover, God can restore him without medicine, and that if he is destined to die, the medicine will be of no avail. No, to*

> *think thus were to tempt God. God has not promised to help us without means; and what God has not promised, we cannot ask of him. Those who despise medicine and die, are guilty of their own murder.*
>
> *2. Yet he must not set his trust upon the physician and his medicine, but upon God; as it is declared to be one of the sins of King Asa, that in his sickness he did not seek God, but the physicians, and trusted them more than God. 2 Chronicles, xvi.12.*
>
> *3. Between these two extremes, the patient must select the golden mean. With his lips and his heart he must pray, and take the medicine in firm reliance upon the helping hand of God; then he may know that there is a blessing upon it.*[8]

PROPER 10

Ephesians 1:3-14 (LBW for 8 Pentecost.)

Ephesians is perhaps the most cosmic book of the Bible. It begins with this statement that God has elected us "in Christ" before the creation of the world for the fulfillment of the divine purpose.

In modern science there is a controversial set of concepts termed "anthropic principles" which express the idea that the development of intelligent life is a central feature of the universe.[9] These range from the well-supported belief that intelligent life couldn't have evolved if the parameters of the universe (e.g., the strengths of the basic forces) were much different from what they are, to the much more speculative suggestion that the development of intelligence is *necessary* for the existence of the universe. (Quantum mechanical ideas about the relationship between observers and physical systems are cited to support such claims.)

The argument of Ephesians is not, of course, based on such ideas. It does, however, provide a theological parallel to anthropic principles which we might label a *the*anthropic principle.

Here it is not merely human beings as a set of intelligent observers who enable the universe to exist and express its purpose. It is humanity indwelt by God, the *theanthropos* Jesus Christ, as the head of a new humanity, who is the creator and the fulfillment of the cosmos.

Karl Barth's understanding of election provides one way to proceed with such considerations, though his view of covenant was too narrowly limited to a relationship between God and humanity. The covenant which is "the internal form of creation"[10] should be seen as a covenant between God and all creation. This is necessary on biblical grounds (see the discussion of Hosea 2:14-20 for 8 Epiphany B) and because of the connections between humanity and the rest of the world which evolutionary theory and ecology describe.

PROPER 12

Psalm 145:10-19; John 6:1-21 (LBW has all of Psalm 145 and John 6:1-15 for 10 Pentecost.)

We have already commented on the Matthean account of the feeding of the 5,000 and the general question of miracles for Proper 13 A. Here one might emphasize that this spectacular feeding by Jesus is not unique. Every day,

> *The eyes of all wait upon you, O LORD,*
> *and you give them their food in due season.*
> *You open wide your hand*
> *and satisfy the needs of every living creature.*
> (Psalm 145:15-16)

Conversely, the feeding of the 5,000 is, for those who know the Old Testament's teaching on creation, like a huge lighted arrow bearing the word "Creator" and pointing to Jesus.

John's account also invites us to connect God's work of feeding all living things through the processes of nature with the Lord's Supper. This is suggested by the word *eucharistesas* in v. 11. In the Eucharist Christ does not remove us from the natural world, but takes up that world with its solar energy, photosynthesis, soil, weather, and genetics into union with himself and with those who eat and drink. *"This* is my body."

PROPER 15

Proverbs 9:1-6; John 6:51-58 (LBW for 13 Pentecost.)

This is the fourth week that the Gospel has dealt with John's account of the feeding of the 5,000 and the following "bread of life" discourse, in which Jesus identifies himself as the living bread from heaven. Today we see that against the backdrop of Wisdom's invitation: "Come, eat of my bread and drink of the wine I have mixed." And that should be thought of together with the role of Wisdom in Proverbs 8.

Wisdom has many aspects in Hebrew thought, ranging from the common sense needed for right living through insight into the secrets of the world to the underlying created order in the universe.[11] It reaches beyond humanity and the world to God. Wisdom is an attribute of God which is personalized so strongly in Proverbs 8 and Wisdom 7 that it prepared the way for the Christian belief in the Word (John 1:1-3) or Wisdom (1 Corinthians 1:30) of God as a person of the Trinity.

This fundamental ordering of the world, a person rather than an abstract principle, is the bread of life who invites us to the banquet. That feast is, first of all, the Eucharist, where Christ is present. But it includes all our eating and drinking and our encounters with the material world structured in accord with the divine Wisdom. The universe is sacramental because of its centering in the remembrance and reactualization of the crucified and risen Wisdom of God.

Wisdom concludes by saying, "Lay aside immaturity [or simpleness], and live, and walk in the way of insight." God calls us to be "wise," not "simple," even if that takes us on the path of skepticism about traditional beliefs. The Judaeo-Christian tradition has been courageous enough to canonize this path in the Book of Ecclesiastes. In Christ, the Wisdom of God, it is possible for us to engage in the most critical studies of theology and natural science without losing our faith.

Psalm 111 is given as an alternative by RCL. For discussion see 4 Epiphany B.

PROPER 16

Ephesians 6:10-20 (LBW for 15 Pentecost.)

In the New Testament, the "holy war" tradition of Israel is transferred to the level of spiritual combat with demonic powers. It is a war in which God has won the decisive victory through the cross of Christ (Colossians 2:15). But battles still go on, as this passage, with its martial imagery, emphasizes.

Language about battles with demonic powers is the clearest example of the use of a mythological worldview in the New Testament, a use with which Bultmann's demythologizing program was intended to deal. He argued that such language makes no sense to people with a modern scientific view of the world. But Bultmann's approach was so concerned with existential encounter and the personal faith of the individual that it provided little encouragement for theological reflection on the scientific understanding of the world. If the full message of the New Testament is to engage us, we have to ask what structures in our scientific and technological existence play the role that the "principalities" and "powers" (v. 12, RSV) did in the first century.

In traditional Christian theology, Satan and the demonic powers are, in essence, *good* because they are creatures of God. There is no "evil God" on the same ontological level as the "good God." But good creatures, who owe their existence to God, become evil if they are turned from their proper role by their own will or the wills of those who have a misplaced trust in them. All creatures have the *possibility* of being evil, like the "angels who did not keep their own position" (Jude 6) of traditional demonology. Money, sex, and church growth can be objects of idolatry even more easily than fallen angels.

In the modern world, science and the technology which science makes available can become objects of ultimate trust, and thus of idolatry. Since these things involve the basic energies of nature, they really can play the role of the demonic in people's lives. When the political powers of the modern state make use of the energies that power the stars in order to enforce their will, we have a close counterpart to the powers which were thought to operate through political structures in the first century. Reliance on military uses of technology today is a soberly demythologized version of the threat of principalities and powers spoken of in Ephesians.

This does not mean that technology, or even military technology, is intrinsically evil. These things are based in God's good creation. Peaceful uses even of nuclear explosives — e.g., for large excavation projects or propulsion of spaceships — have been contemplated. It is the use to which such devices are put, and the degree of reliance placed on them, which determines whether they are good or demonic.

There may be technological ways of combatting the evils of technology. The best way to solve environmental problems brought about by some uses of technology is not necessarily to abandon technology. Aggression may sometimes be appropriately countered by military means, as the "justifiable war" tradition argues.

But the deepest Christian responses to threats posed by principalities and powers are those which have the character of God's decisive victory through the cross. Our text tells us to defend ourselves with paradoxical armor — truth, righteousness, peace, faith, and salvation. The only offensive weapon is the Spirit, and that is not a possession which is under our control. Instead, we are to be under the Spirit's guidance.

This suggests that, in combats with the powers of evil, we are more the weapons which God makes use of than we are warriors.

A selection of verses from 1 Kings 8 is given as an alternative by RCL. For discussion see Proper 4 C.

PROPER 18

Isaiah 35:4-7a (LBW for 16 Pentecost. See the discussion of vv. 1-10 for 3 Advent A.)

Mark 7:24-37 (LBW has vv. 31-37 for 16 Pentecost.)

This is one of the more remarkable healing stories in the gospels. It is not said explicitly that the man had been deaf from birth, but that is suggested by the fact that his deafness is connected with a speech impediment. In those days a person who couldn't hear would never learn to speak, and so would never learn human language. Even if there were no mental defect, the person would be under a severe handicap because of the difficulty of formulating concepts. Jesus is then doing more than just giving the ability to hear sounds or to make them. He is giving the man the gift of language and even of thought. It is no exaggeration that Jesus "has done everything well."

PROPER 20

James 3:13—4:3, 7-8a (LBW has 3:16—4:6 for 18 Pentecost.)

James identifies "earthly" wisdom as sensual and demonic. Thus he challenges much of the Hebrew Wisdom tradition, which held that the pursuit of knowledge (including what we would call "science") is good, as long as the source of all wisdom and knowledge, God, is recognized and worshipped.

(See discussion for 5 Epiphany A.) Passages such as this can be linked to the mistrust of science which has sometimes existed in the history of the Church, a mistrust which has often been unhealthy. But it is salutary to challenge those who place blind faith in science and those who ignore the fact that science is, after all, a human activity, and therefore subject to human limitations.

PROPER 21

James 4:7—5:6 (This is the LBW Second Lesson for 19 Pentecost. RCL omits the verses discussed here.)

Verses 13-17 are a reminder needed especially in a scientific age: the future belongs to God, not to us.

We are able to make accurate forecasts of the future. Eclipses can be predicted many years in advance. Even phenomena qualitatively different from those ever seen before can be predicted. In the early nineteenth century, when the wave theory of light was being debated, the French scientist Poisson showed mathematically that it predicted a tiny bright spot in the center of the shadow of a circular obstacle. He gave that as an argument *against* the wave theory, since "everybody knew" that there was no such spot. But when somebody looked for it, "Poisson's spot" was there! It is now cited in *support* of the wave theory. Poisson had been able to predict the future, but hadn't believed his own prediction.

Many other examples of scientific prognostication could be given. Even when we can't make precise predictions of individual events because of the complexity of the systems we have to deal with and the incompleteness of our information, we can make statistical forecasts. We can't say *which* of the multi-trillions of atomic nuclei in a sample of radium will decay in the next minute, but we can say *how many* will. Insurance companies can use actuarial tables to predict how many people in a certain population will die in the next year.

Both the order in the world which makes such predictions possible and the ability of the human mind to grasp that order are gifts without which human life would not be possible. Imagine what the world would be like if it operated on continual unpredictable miracles — if we didn't know when the sun would rise tomorrow, which substances were poisonous and which nutritious, or whether heat would flow from hot to cold or cold to hot. It would be a nightmare.

The world has an underlying rational pattern, and we are able to discover parts of that pattern and thus know part of the future. We know the future well enough to have no excuse if we are caught napping by some easily foreseen event. The assignment *is* due next Tuesday, it always takes at least twenty minutes to get across town to where your next appointment is, and the signs of your friend's drinking problem were there for anyone to see. We can make budgets and estimate the traffic load on the bridge we're designing.

And yet, the situations of real human lives are so complex that we cannot predict with certainty just what will happen. Recent scientific studies of what has come to be called (not too appropriately) "chaos" have brought out the fact that the development of many systems is very sensitive to their "initial conditions," and in practice cannot be predicted with certainty.[12] The earth's weather systems are a good example of this: It really is true that the flapping of a butterfly's wings in Asia today can bring about significant changes in the weather in New York next month.

The future is in the hands of God, not as one who continually "intervenes" in the world but as one who has made the world with enough flexibility to allow the working out of his will. It is a simple confession of that which James urges. Make the best plans you can, but with the understanding that this is the way things will turn out "if the Lord wishes.".

PROPER 22

Psalm 8 is given as an alternative by RCL. For discussion see Trinity C.

PROPER 23

Psalm 90:12-17 (LBW for 21 Pentecost. See the discussion for Proper 28 A.)

Amos 5:6-15 (LBW For 21 Pentecost.) Verses 8 and 9 should not be omitted.

Amos shows a strong concern for social justice throughout this book. This is because *God* is concerned about justice. And that is really a remarkable idea: the God who created the stars (v. 8) cares passionately about the treatment of the poor in Samaria. When we consider the creation of the universe and the ways in which God is at work in stellar evolution, we are not to think of a God different from the one who insists that the widow and the orphan be treated fairly.

Today we recognize justice in environmental matters as part of this concern. Pollution and wastage of resources can have far-reaching consequences, perhaps as mind-boggling as the stretches of interstellar space. There are various ways in which the preacher might tie together the grandeur of the universe and the far-reaching implications of our stewardship of creation. The wastes from our power plants which utilize nuclear fission will continue to be radioactive long after our individual lives end, and indeed far longer than any civilization or even the whole of recorded human history has lasted. (The half-life of plutonium-239 is about 24,000 years.) If we are to use nuclear energy, our stewardship must be planned not just on a short-term basis but on a geological time scale.

PROPER 24

Psalm 104:1-9, 24, 35c and **Job 38:1-7 [34-41]** are given as alternatives by RCL. For discussion see, respectively, Pentecost A and Proper 7 B.

PROPER 25

Mark 10:46-52 (LBW for 23 Pentecost.)

Jesus' words to Bartimaeus, whose sight he has just restored, are repeated in a number of the accounts of his healings: "Your faith has made you well." This may tempt us to overuse the word "psychosomatic" as an explanation of apparently miraculous healings. And yet the human spirit is a crucial factor in all healing. When a patient has simply given up on life, all the high-tech medicine in the world may not be able to heal. On the other hand, the patient's simple determination to recover can apparently seize the powers which medicine offers and make them effective.

One of our parishioners, eighty years old, had surgery for the replacement of one knee. Without going to a rehabilitation center she returned to her two-story house. With the help of friends who shopped and cleaned for her, she took care of herself and within six months had recovered almost complete use of her knee. Then, after moving to a retirement community, she had the other knee replaced. But within a week after her return, she broke a hip, fell to the floor, and had to go back to the hospital. A setback like that could have been the end, but after a week in rehabilitation therapy she was back in her apartment and was soon walking with a walker.

That kind of spirit and will to be healthy is the unknown quality that medical professionals long to have in a patient. And God is the creator of that intangible aspect of human nature as well as of our bodily realities. Jesus' words, "Your faith has made you well," have profound medical *and* theological meaning.

PROPER 26

Deuteronomy 6:1-9 (LBW for 24 Pentecost.)

Verse 4, the *Shema,* is Israel's basic confession of faith in one God. Yahweh, who creates and sustains the universe, who keeps it and each individual creature, who saves and sanctifies, is one, and is alone to be the ultimate object of trust.

In most of the cultures surrounding Israel there were many gods and goddesses, one in charge of fertility, one governing the sea, one to be asked for help in war, and so on. Even if there were one supreme deity, such a polytheistic view meant a fragmentation of reality. The universe was made up of different parts subject to different rules. One couldn't expect to find general laws which would apply throughout the universe, or relationships between the laws which might apply in different parts of it. A comprehensive understanding of the world, such as modern science aims at, would be impossible.

The idea of a unified government of the world can undergird such an ambitious view of science. Of course that is not necessarily the same as the belief that the one God is Yahweh, who brought Israel out of Egypt. There would be no scientific or philosophical compulsion to identify such a sole governor of the world with the Holy Trinity. However, the belief in the unity of God which eventually made possible the rise of modern science was that which lies at the root of the biblical tradition.

Polytheism in the traditional sense is not a major force in the western world today, though there are various attempts to *re*mythologize the world. But the problem of the fragmentation of reality is certainly with us. We see this in the mental compartmentalization which many people use to deal with religion, ethics, and science. Many people actually "know" that dinosaurs walked the earth millions of years ago, but on Sunday morning convince themselves that the dinosaurs were drowned in the Noachic flood. Real belief in the unity of God doesn't fit very well with such doublethink. An ongoing science-theology dialogue ought to be one of the main results of a genuine belief that the one true God is the one whose works we encounter in scientific study as well as in Scripture.

Ruth 1:1-18 is given as an alternative by RCL. For discussion see Proper 23 C.

PROPER 27

Hebrews 9:23-28 (LBW for 25 Pentecost.) We begin a verse earlier than the lectionaries.

The idea that the things of this world are copies of heavenly realities has been common and influential. In western thought it is often associated with Plato, and we may simply use the term "platonism" for it here. But such thinking was also prevalent in the ancient Near East independent of the Greek philosopher. On the basis of the command to Moses (Exodus 25:40) that the tabernacle and its appointments were to be made according to the pattern shown him on Mount Sinai (Hebrews 8:5), the writer to the Hebrews developed the idea of Christ presenting his sacrifice in the *real* heavenly tabernacle as the high priest would do in shadow fashion each year on *Yom Kippur.*

The platonic theory can be fatal to belief in the goodness of creation and study of the material world. If the heavenly realm is the only important one, the earthly may be neglected. But if kept in a subordinate role by belief in the importance of the material world demanded by the doctrines of creation and the Incarnation, the platonic way of looking at things is helpful. It stresses the idea that the material world corresponds to a rational pattern, and the search for laws of nature can then be seen as an attempt to approximate that pattern by means of mathematics. The influence of the platonic theory can be seen in the writings of a number of modern physicists, the clearest example being Heisenberg's scientific autobiography.[13]

The thread connecting a search for natural laws based on mathematical symmetry with the picture of the atonement in Hebrews is slender. But the connection is there, and may at least be useful for illustrative purposes.

PROPER 28

Psalm 111 is appointed by LBW for 27 Pentecost. See the discussion for 4 Epiphany B.

Mark 13:1-8 is the RCL Gospel, while LBW gives vv. 24-31 for 27 Pentecost. See the discussion of Mark 13:24-37 for 1 Advent B.

CHRIST THE KING

Revelation 1:4b-8 (See the discussion for 3 Easter C.)

John 18:33-37

"What is truth?" Pilate demands. Discovering truth about the world is the whole point of the scientific endeavor. What are the constituents of the world, how do they behave, and what has been their history? How can we get reliable knowledge about the world, and how do we test our ideas? What is true, what do we mean by saying that it's true, and how do we know it's true?

Pilate's question is the same but not the same, an example of Johannine ambiguity and misunderstanding. On one level, it is our question about truth, flavored with the cynicism of a Roman politician. But it is a mistake to think that Jesus would have answered Pilate's question — would have told him the truth in the form of some wise sayings or correct information — if Pilate had only been willing to wait. The terrible irony is that Truth with a capital T is standing right in front of him. The one of whom the governor asks the question is the one who has said, "I am the way, and the truth, and the life" (John 14:6). That Pilate is not of the truth, that he is not open to God's truth, is shown by the fact that he does not recognize Jesus (18:37 — cf. 10:3-5).

Our experience of the world brings us into contact with truth in the form of facts about ourselves and our surroundings, and we try to respond with true theories about the world — or at least truer theories than those of our predecessors. But as we penetrate to deeper strata of reality, we have to reckon not just with true things but with personal truth in the person of the creator, the one who stands before Pilate (John 1:3). That forces us to realize that even in purely scientific investigation of the world there is a personal element — the love of truth, the honesty, the *feel* for the world that great scientists have. That is why Michael Polanyi spoke of "personal knowledge" as an important aspect of the scientific endeavor.[14]

Christians have no head start over others in their attempts to do science. The world is knowable *etsi deus non daretur,* "though God were not given." But Christians, unlike Pilate, know the name of the truth who is at the heart of the world.

Endnotes

1. A few years ago the American Scientific Affiliation sold a note card with a picture of this inscription.

2. Colin A. Russell, *Cross-Currents: Interactions Between Science and Faith* (Eerdmans, Grand Rapids MI, 1985), p. 211.

3. St. Augustine, *The Enchiridion on Faith, Hope and Love* (Henry Regnery, Chicago, 1961), Sections XI-XV, pp. 11-17.

4. Lewis, *Miracles*, pp. 115-116. An apparent typographical error has been corrected here.

5. Paul J. Nahin, *Time Machines: Time Travel in Physics, Metaphysics, and Science Fiction* (American Institute of Physics, New York, 1993).

6. NRSV's "mortals" is unfortunate here, since the next verse says "Death will be no more."

7. Kent S. Knutson, *His Only Son Our Lord* (Augsburg, Minneapolis, 1966), Chapter IV.

8. John Frederick Stark, *Daily Hand-Book* (I. Kohler, Philadelphia, 1855), pp. 297-298.

9. The case for anthropic principles is set out in detail in John D. Barrow and Frank J. Tipler, *The Anthropic Cosmological Principle* (Oxford, New York, 1986).

10. Karl Barth, *Church Dogmatics* (T. & T. Clark, Edinburgh, 1936-1968), III/I, pp. 96-99 & 229-233.

11. Gerhard von Rad, *Wisdom in Israel* (Abingdon, New York, 1972).

12. James Gleick, *Chaos: Making a New Science* (Penguin, New York, 1987).

13. Werner Heisenberg, *Physics and Beyond* (Harper & Row, New York, 1971).

14. Michael Polanyi, *Personal Knowledge* (Harper & Row, New York, 1964).

Year C

1 ADVENT

Luke 21:25-36

Rachel Carson's *Silent Spring,* published in 1962, was for its generation a sign that the end of the world was near. But then so were some of the books by the muckrakers at the turn of the century. Changes in weather patterns and rising oceans are other signs that we view with alarm. Some look upon any conflict in the Middle East, like the recent Gulf War, as a potential Armageddon.

Christians may properly view such things as signs, not only that Jesus will come again to judge the world, but also that he is continually present, judging and calling to repentance. One of the themes of Advent is a call to prepare the way of the Lord, for the coming of Jesus Christ to live within us, by repenting and changing our actions. It is a call to turn around our behavior. Among other things, we are to change from being wasters to being recyclers, and from being polluters to being those who clean up air and water. Jesus calls us to repentance for public and common sinfulness as well as for private and personal disobedience.

Ecologists and all who help us to care for the earth and its resources, and sociologists and others who help us to live together, have a lot to tell us about the repentance we need to experience and the stewardship we are to exercise as our Advent preparation while we wait for God to return to walk with us. Will that return find us hiding from the judgment we fear, like Adam and Eve? Or will we be able to "stand up and raise [our] heads, because [our] redemption is drawing near" (v. 28)?

2 ADVENT

Malachi 3:1-4

Science-based technology is a pervasive feature of our culture. People from the time of this "messenger," transported to our time, would be astounded at the things our technologies can do. But the existence of technology itself would not be strange to them. They knew about practical metallurgy and other ways of changing the world, largely by trial and error and through tradition rather than through systematic understanding of the world. The later development of such craft traditions, however, was one of the things which made science possible. The Bible traces these traditions back to the earliest periods of the human race (Genesis 4:22).

Prophets like Malachi could use the technology of their time as "sermon illustrations." The metallurgical metaphor is also developed in other places in the Bible, such as 1 Peter 1:7. Preachers today can do more than simply repeat the Bible's technological metaphors. They can go on to use images taken from today's cutting-edge technologies to communicate the gospel. Heart transplants suggest a modern metaphor which could be used with verses like Ezekiel 11:19 and 18:31, which speak of God giving people a new heart.

1 CHRISTMAS

Psalm 148 is discussed for this Sunday in Year A.

Psalm 111 is assigned for this Sunday each year by LBW. We treat it for 4 Epiphany B.

Hebrews 2:10-18, the Second Lesson in LBW, is assigned to this Sunday in Year A in RCL. See the discussion there.

Luke 2:41-52

The comments for this Sunday's Gospel for Year B, focusing on Luke 2:40, are also applicable to v. 52 here.

2 EPIPHANY

Psalm 36:5-10

> *For with you is the well of life,*
> *and in your light we see light.*

It is fascinating to see how the image of "light" is used in Scripture. Sometimes the word refers to "ordinary" light, sometimes to spiritual or mental illumination, and sometimes it isn't possible to separate the meanings. "Light" is a metaphor for God's glory *(kabhodh)*, but then in Revelation 21:23 the metaphorical light seems to get back its "ordinary" meaning when the glory of God takes the place of sun and moon.

Why the quotation marks around "ordinary"? Simply because there is nothing ordinary about light as a physical phenomenon. It provides most of our signals from the external world (and almost all those from beyond the earth). The study of light has been the impetus for many of the major developments in physics, such as relativity and quantum theory. Advanced forms of life depend, in one way or another, on photosynthesis by green plants, so that there is an intimate relationship between light and life. (Cf. John 1:4.) While many biblical uses of "light" are symbolic, scientific descriptions of light have a metaphorical quality as well. Light is a real phenomenon obeying definite laws and bringing about definite effects. But when we come to say what light *is*, whether we try to picture it as a stream of particles or as a wave disturbance, or content ourselves with writing down the equations which describe its behavior, we are using symbolic language. (See the comments on Maxwell's equations for Proper 4 B.) It is no accident that *poets* often make use of light imagery.

The Bible doesn't tell us about the physical nature of light. It can't be used as the basis for lectures on physical optics or photochemistry anymore than a book on telescope design can proclaim salvation. Both science and theology provide us with metaphors of light and darkness (though neither is *exclusively* metaphorical); it is worthwhile to explore ways in which different metaphors can enrich one another.

A preacher is not limited to repeating the Bible's uses of the light image. The different roles which light plays in modern science can be used to carry on the biblical tradition. The process of photosynthesis is an absolutely crucial connection between light and life like that spoken of in today's Psalm, and this may suggest metaphors for God as the source of life. The fact that Einstein's relativity theory gave the speed of light an absolute character (as we discussed in the commentary on John 14:1-14 for 5 Easter A) suggests one way of illustrating God's absoluteness.

3 EPIPHANY

Isaiah 61:1-6 is LBW's First Lesson for this Sunday. See the discussion for 3 Advent B.

1 Corinthians 12:12-31a (LBW has vv. 12-21 and 26-27 for this Sunday and 12:27—13:13 for the next.)

This is Paul's most detailed development of the image of the Body of Christ. The Church is seen as an organic unity of members with different gifts and functions, whose head is Christ. J.A.T. Robinson traced this concept to Paul's Damascus Road experience and the revelation that in persecuting Christians he was persecuting Christ himself.[1]

Teilhard de Chardin used this idea in his discussions of the theological significance of evolution. He pointed out that a major step in evolution had been the development of multicellular organisms and then of creatures with diversified organs. This meant that specialized tissues could develop for structural purposes, sensors, signal transmission, assimilation of nutrition, and other needs. Because these different parts of a body are united and dependent upon one another, they can fully develop their unique functions. A heart can be a much better heart when it only pumps blood and depends upon other organs for other things. Thus this development in evolution did not mean homogenization of organs but their opposite, diversification. As Teilhard put it succinctly, "union differentiates."[2]

That is precisely the point Paul is making here about the Church as the Body of Christ. There are different abilities and functions, and the body achieves its full potential when each is recognized and honored. (Cf. Ephesians 4:13.)

Reader's Digest used to have a series of articles on the different parts of the body, told in the "first person" by the different organs — "I Am Joe's Heart" and so on. The preacher could use this idea for a story sermon on the Body of Christ, allowing different members to speak about their functions. Some parts of the body to which we give little thought are actually essential to our well-being. Or perhaps the whole idea of the cooperation and interdependence of different members could be explored in story fashion with conversations among the different members.

We can go on to speak of the Body of Christ as *the next stage in evolution*. The future of human evolution has received varied treatments from different writers. Nietzsche proclaimed "the superman" (but definitely not the super*woman*), and science fiction writers have had a field day picturing advanced or degenerated products of evolution beyond us. The possibility of human genetic engineering seems to put us in charge of evolution, so that we can choose the superhuman that we wish. All of these speculations have in mind the development of the individual human being beyond its present capabilities.

Teilhard's image, taken from Saint Paul, is quite different. The superpersonal union of believers with God Incarnate is the real evolutionary future, a qualitative change in the course of evolution as radical as the development of multicellular organisms a billion years ago. It is the Christian Church which is the new humanity.

That idea may arouse concern. It might suggest a completely uniform society where everyone is the same as everyone else, and there are no personal boundaries between individuals — the kind of thing family systems theory calls "undifferentiated ego mass." ("Slime mold" is a good biological illustration with a suitably repulsive name!) And Teilhard did sometimes show too much fascination with the totalitarian regimes of his time.

But the basic point which we noted about the body, and Paul's use of this image, argues against such ideas. "Union differentiates." The real body is not just a lot of identical cells or organs which share the same space, but different types of cells and organs which are able to operate together just because they are different and interdependent. "So it is with Christ" — with God's new humanity.

Just as each of us is fully human only in human community, the Body of Christ is fully what God intends for it to be only in communion with the rest of creation. There is an inescapable ecological dimension to the calling of the Body of Christ.

4 EPIPHANY

Jeremiah 1:4-10

In the prophetic tradition, the technological activities of *building* and *planting* were metaphors for the human vocation. (See, for example, Isaiah 65:21; Jeremiah 31:28, 35:7; Ezekiel 28:26; and Amos 9:14.) Jeremiah's call uses such language:

> *See, today I appoint you over nations and over kingdoms,*
> *to pluck up and to pull down,*
> *to destroy and to overthrow,*
> *to build and to plant.*
>
> (v. 10)

Thus the prophet's role parallels that of humanity.

Jeremiah continually had to denounce human sinfulness, the tendencies to make "mere flesh" our strength and to "boast" of our wisdom (17:5 and 9:23). Sin is often displayed in our use of technology, upon which we rely for our present security and hope for the future. The exemplar of this theme is the Tower of Babel, where the people begin to "build ourselves a city, and a tower with its top in the heavens, [and] make a name for ourselves" (Genesis 11:4). (See the commentary for Pentecost C.)

The prophets picture God's ultimate response to such sin in terms of the coming "Day of the LORD," when God will overturn the sinful worldly order. On that day no human technology will be able to stand against God's righteous wrath. (See the commentary for Proper 28 A on Zephaniah 1:7, 12-18.)

But this is not the last word on technology or God's purpose. The prophetic vision is also one of redemption and renewal. The metaphor of building and planting describes a human vocation responsive to the will of God. With it we can preach the hope for renewal and the responsibility to develop technology which is appropriate to the will of God. (For a discussion of "appropriate technology" see the commentary for 1 Advent A.) Technology of redemption and renewal is technology which promotes justice, sustainability, and participation.

Preaching this vision is a call to responsible life now, not at some time in the distant future. We are called by God to build and plant in our Age. Thus our technological being can be viewed as part of our God-willed human vocation.

7 EPIPHANY

1 Corinthians 15:35-38, 42-50

The Christian hope is the resurrection of the body. It is not just a mental or spiritual part of a woman or man which is given the promise of eternal life in Christ but the whole person. That puts the Christian faith in an adversarial position against common ideas of an afterlife. An immortal soul was all right for Paul's philosophically inclined audience at Athens, but "when they heard of the resurrection of the dead, some scoffed" (Acts 17:32). Many people today would join them.

"How are the dead raised? With what kind of body do they come?" There is a basic foolishness about such questions if they fail to recognize that the resurrection comes only by passing through death, and if rational explanations of the process are demanded as a precondition of belief. But Paul does go on here, not so much to explain the nature of the resurrection body as to provide some analogies which can sustain faith.

It is not simply the body which died which is raised. Resuscitation of a corpse is described in, for example, the story of the raising of Lazarus, but this idea is inadequate to describe the resurrection of Christ, who "being raised from the dead will never die again" (Romans 6:9), and the future resurrection consequent upon that. Paul says that the body which dies is like the "seed" of the resurrection body, the same though different. (See the discussion of Philippians 3:20-21 for 2 Lent C.)

There is one concern in this area to which modern science can give an answer. Some people considering organ or tissue donation worry about the effect this might have on bodily integrity in the resurrection. That can be a problem if one has a common-sense understanding of material identity. How can the same matter be part of two bodies in the resurrection? In fact, that argument provided a classic argument against resurrection in terms of the problem posed by a person eaten by cannibals with which Augustine and other theologians attempted to deal.

The donation of an organ is an act of self-giving which is certainly consistent with the example of Christ. If there is any lack in the risen body of one who has donated an organ, it can be compared with the wounds which the risen Christ still bears. This is not something to be afraid of. But that does not answer the question about material identity. Can two bodies contain some of the same atoms?

With the quantum mechanical understanding of matter, the whole concept of "the same atoms" is radically different from what common sense suggests. Particles of the same kind — electrons, protons, carbon-12 atoms, etc. — are *completely* identical in quantum theory. There is no way of telling them apart. Heisenberg's uncertainty principle says that we cannot follow particles carefully enough to be able to say which is which after they interact. The question of whether or not "the same atoms" are in a body therefore loses its meaning. We can only talk about whether or not the same pattern of atoms is found. The problem of material identity posed by transplants or cannibalism turns out in the light of quantum theory to be a non-problem.

Of course what has been said here should not be understood as giving any scientific "proof" of the resurrection. But it does mean that, when the modern scientific understanding of matter is taken into account, proclamation of the resurrection can be made with some intellectual integrity.

This is a matter of considerable practical importance. Organ donation can be literally a matter of life and death, and there is a serious shortage of vital organs available for transplants. People should not be deflected from allowing donations because of an inadequate theology of the resurrection. It will be too late if pastors wait to address such issues in an emergency room waiting area. They need to be dealt with in Christian education and (because many adults do not attend Sunday School classes) in sermons.

8 EPIPHANY

Isaiah 55:10-13 is given as an alternative by RCL. For discussion see Proper 10 A.

9 EPIPHANY

RCL provides readings for churches which do not observe this as Transfiguration Sunday. For this year the Gospel is **Luke 7:1-10**, which we discuss for Proper 4 C.

1 LENT

Deuteronomy 26:1-11 (LBW has vv. 5-10.)

The "historical credo" of Israel expresses the faith that God is active in the events of history. It is the ancestor of the phrases in the ecumenical creeds which speak of Christ having suffered "under Pontius Pilate." The events of salvation history are phenomena of the material universe.

The events of the historical credo are not just the salvific ones like the Exodus. They are also the events of everyday providence: the occasion for this confession is a celebration of harvest (26:2). It is God who gives "the fruit of the ground." A belief in creation which sees God at work through the processes of agriculture is part of this early biblical creed.

2 LENT

Philippians 3:17—4:1

The King James Version says in vv. 20-21, "We look for the Saviour, the Lord Jesus Christ: Who shall change our vile body, that it may be fashioned like unto his glorious body." "Vile" is a very negative word, and RSV's "lowly" seems more pleasant. (NRSV's literal "body of our humiliation" is clumsy.) But perhaps this reflects the ambiguity which we often do feel about our bodies. We are "fearfully and wonderfully made" (Psalm 139:14), and yet anyone who has witnessed an autopsy also knows how fitting Luther's characterization of himself as "a miserable bag of worms" can be. Human physiology is awe-inspiring in its complexity and efficiency, but it takes a strong stomach to deal with some parts of it.

Our bodies are "lowly" in some ways, but biblical faith doesn't express shame at *being* bodily creatures, as at least one non-Christian philosopher did. Instead it speaks with Paul of the change, but not the annihilation, of bodily existence, its transformation into the likeness of the risen Christ. Physical reality is to be hallowed in order to share in God's final future. With all the doubts Protestants have felt about the veneration of bodies, or parts of bodies, of saints, they ought to remember the solid kernel of truth in such practices. The flesh *is* capable of sanctification. That is why Dante could speak of "the glorious and holy flesh,"[3] and why the mathematician Jakob Bernoulli had a geometric figure, the logarithmic spiral, which appears in many guises in mathematics, engraved on his tombstone with the words *eadem mutata resurgo,* "I arise the same though changed."[4]

5 LENT

Isaiah 43:14-21 (We begin two verses earlier than the lectionaries.)

God's self-identification in Second Isaiah is as the creator and the redeemer of Israel, and therefore the One on whom the entire universe depends for its existence and well-being. The promise here is that God's work of saving Israel will continue, and in fact that there will be new salvific acts which will dwarf those of old. God's creative involvement with the world is ongoing. This foreshadows the New Testament themes of the identity of creator and redeemer in Christ, and the work of Christ as new creation. Salvation cannot be separated from creation, as if the latter were merely a preliminary to the former.

This passage is a reminder to preachers. Proclamation of the gospel must include proclamation that the redeemer is the creator.

EASTER

Exodus 15:1-11 is LBW's First Lesson for this Sunday. In RCL and LBW it is part of the response to the fourth reading for the Easter Vigil.

The Exodus is the basic saving event of the Old Testament, as the death and resurrection of Jesus are of the New. God is identified for Israel as the One who brought them out of Egypt.

It is interesting to see how this deliverance is described in the Song of Moses, and perhaps a little surprising to see it connected with the wind. Verse 10 in the poetic celebration recalls the more prosaic statement of Exodus 14:21: "The LORD drove the sea back by a strong east wind all night, and turned the sea into dry land." The distinction between "miraculous" and "natural" events which seems obvious to the modern mind was not assumed by ancient Israel. The wind is *God's* wind (v. 10), the blast of God's nostrils (v. 8). It is at God's command, and accomplishes God's purpose. But there is no reason to think that it was not in principle describable by the laws which characterize other meteorological phenomena. God may work through natural processes in the special events of saving history, just as in the everyday things which maintain the world.

2 EASTER

Revelation 1:4-8 (See the discussion of Revelation for the following Sunday.)

3 EASTER

Revelation 5:11-14

The Second Lesson for each Sunday after Easter this year is from this strange Book of Revelation, a book whose picture of the world seems in many ways at odds with the scientific view of things. Some of the difficulty disappears when we grasp the basic theme: in a time of great difficulty for Christians, when the whole world seems in turmoil, God is still "the Almighty" (4:8). This does not mean "almighty" in the crude sense of being able to achieve arbitrary purposes by raw power. God is, rather, almighty through "the Lamb that was slaughtered" (v. 12). Revelation shows God in charge of world history, and does this in part by alternating between the drama going on on earth and the scenes like that in our text of rejoicing in heaven for God's already accomplished victory.

The heavenly choir which sings the praise of "the one seated on the throne" and "the Lamb" contains angels and elders and the "living creatures."[5] "Every creature in heaven," but also those "on earth and under the earth and in the seas, and all that is in them" praise God. The whole universe praises God, as in Psalm 148 or the Song of the Three, because all are to share in God's salvation. (Cf. also Philippians 2:10.) There is no part of creation too insignificant to share in the ultimate worship of God.

5 EASTER

Revelation 21:1-6 (LBW has vv. 1-5.)

There is not as much in the Bible as one might think about "going to heaven." In the present passage, near the culmination of the cosmic drama of Revelation, the motion is in the opposite direction. "The holy city, the new Jerusalem" is coming down to the new earth (v. 1), and God's dwelling will be with humanity.

The whole course of Scripture has prepared for this, from the consecrating presence of the Spirit in Genesis 1:2 through God's wilderness journey with Israel and promise to place the divine "name" in the Temple at Jerusalem. God already "came down from heaven" to dwell with humanity in the flesh (John 1:14), taking the place of the Temple (John 2:21). Now this movement reaches its climax in the descent of the holy city, whose "temple is the Lord God Almighty and the Lamb" (21:22).

This has clear implications for the way we view and treat the world. The physical universe is to be transformed in ways that we cannot now fully grasp. We can understand the world as it now is by scientific means because we are on the "downstream" side of God's original creative work. We are not in that position with respect to the new creation except as we experience it proleptically in the risen Christ in Word and sacraments. The earth, like humanity, will be transformed in the resurrection — but it is to be a new *earth*. Like the human body, it will "arise the same, though changed." (Cf. 2 Lent C.)

And so the nonhuman part of the world is not to be seen as dispensable stage settings. It shares in the hope for newness, a hope finally free from the threat of destruction because "the sea was no more." The "chaos monsters" of the old creation myths (e.g., Psalm 89:10) will be gone for good.

Psalm 148 is given as an alternative by RCL. For discussion see 1 Christmas A.

6 EASTER

Psalm 67

The first part of the sixth verse speaks of the produce of the earth in a way which any atheistic materialist could accept. It is "the earth" which brings forth food (with the help of solar energy, etc.) through natural processes. But the psalmist sees God as the One who provides such blessings. God is the one who, in Genesis 1, commands the earth and the waters to bring forth life, and who has been sustaining the universe in that way since the beginning of time. It is not too hard to imagine a God who makes things. It is more amazing that God makes things make themselves!

Acts 14:8-18 is LBW's First Lesson for this Sunday.

This is the first clear confrontation in Scripture of the Christian message with pagan religious practices, and one of the few appeals in the Bible to natural theology. Polytheism, as we pointed out for Proper 26 B, means dissolution of the world into separate domains governed by different deities and obeying different rules. Over against that, Barnabas and Paul proclaim that there is *one* God, the *living* God, who has created all things.

Revelation 21:10, 22—22:5 (LBW has 21:10-14, 22-23. The former selection is preferable.)

Much of Revelation has pictured the rebellious battle of earthly powers against God, and their defeat. The "kings of the earth" were destroyed by the Word and the heavenly armies in 19:17-21. But then, rather surprisingly (but not completely so if we realize that this book is not about the chronological ordering of future events), here they come riding into the heavenly city bringing "the glory and the honor of the nations."[6]

History matters! What happens in the world, even the smallest bit of good accomplished, will somehow be brought into God's ultimate reality. There is good reason to understand the world and use what we know to improve it. This present life is not only a time of testing but a time to contribute to the glory and honor of the nations. After you've taken a test and gotten the result, you can throw the paper away. When a new experiment is carried out, when a new computer is built or surgery succeeds, the results are kept. So it is with the world. Only we must recall that the final evaluation is God's. We are not the final judges of what belongs to the glory and honor of the nations and what is their shame.

PENTECOST

Psalm 104:25-35, 37 (See commentary for Year A.)

Genesis 11:1-9

The shadow of that hyddeous strength
Sax myle and more it is of length.

Those lines of Sir David Lindsay on the Tower of Babel are on the title page of C.S. Lewis' novel *That Hideous Strength,* the concluding book of the "space trilogy" in which, half a century ago, he argued against what he saw as dangerous and dehumanizing aspects of the modern scientific view of the world.[7] Lewis' picture of science is somewhat dated now: "The National Institute for Co-ordinated Experiments" is a minor league operation in comparison with today's research establishments.

Yet the basic warning remains valid. Science and technology can play the role of the Tower of Babel if they become our means of exalting ourselves and usurping the position of God. Humanity senses its insecurity and the possibility that it will be broken up. But, confident of their abilities, people try to provide their own security by their technical capabilities. At the time Lewis was writing his book, the nation which had had the most advanced science in the world was trying to protect its "racial purity" by devising efficient scientific ways to exterminate the Jews, and was looking forward to Hitler's grandiose architectural visions.

Technology itself, as part of God's gift to humanity in creation, needs no apologies. And yet, like all gifts, it can be misused. The builders of the Tower were not — at least from what we can tell from the story in Genesis — consciously trying to oust God. They don't even mention God! They might be at home in our post-Christian era, in which many intellectuals don't even think that Christianity is worth arguing with.

The failure of Project Babel comes about because people with their single-minded focus on the technical endeavor are unable to communicate with one another. Language has become divisive instead of unitive. And perhaps it is not too farfetched to see the misuse of language in social and political propaganda, dishonesty in advertising, and the appalling state of scientific prose as symptoms of the Babel syndrome in our culture.

The Pentecost story of Acts 2 reverses Babel. Through the Holy Spirit we are able to talk to one another, and the gospel can be communicated to all people in their own tongue.

TRINITY

Psalm 8

The majesty of God in the universe is seen by those who believe it to be God's handiwork, even "infants and children," those incapable of following sophisticated cosmological arguments for God's existence. To say it is God's glory which is chanted by the heavens, and not the glory of the human discoverer or an autonomous universe, is an expression of faith. On the other hand, the heavens themselves, without faith in God, can be fearsome. "The silence of those interstellar spaces fills me with dread," said Pascal, a profound Christian who was unimpressed by arguments of natural theology.

Indeed, what is a mere human being to be considered by God in the vastness of the cosmos? That question comes in the middle of the Psalm, at the end of a descent from "O LORD our Lord, how exalted is your name in all the world!" And there follows a reascent, through statements about the dominion God has given to humanity, to that same praise of the God of Israel. Humanity is placed at the center of a chiastic structure, with God as beginning and end.

If our universe were just a little different, life would not have developed. As one example, while most substances contract when they freeze, water, which is crucial for life as we know it, *expands* on freezing. Thus ice floats. If this were not so, lakes would freeze from the bottom up, aquatic animals would not be able to survive winter, and higher forms of life would probably not have developed on earth. In this and in many other ways, the universe seems to be rather finely "tuned" to allow the development of intelligent life.

Some scientists have seen this as more than a series of coincidences. They have proposed "anthropic principles" which say that intelligent life has a special status in the universe, and may even be crucial for the *existence* of the cosmos.[8] Such ideas remain controversial, and other scientists reject them.

The Bible does see the human race as having a crucial place in the universe. It does not, however, simply place humanity in the starring role in the universal drama. That role is filled by humanity indwelt by God, human nature "enpersoned" in the person of the Word. Thus the writer to the Hebrews extends the thought of the psalmist by seeing these verses fulfilled in Jesus (Hebrews 2:5-9). Our discussion of Colossians 1:13-20 for Christ the King Sunday of this year expands further upon that theme.

Proverbs 8:1-4, 22-31 (LBW has only vv. 22-31.)

This text has been a center of controversy, but it is also one rich with meaning for our understanding of God's relationship with the world. In verse 22 Wisdom says the LORD "created [KJV, "possessed"] me at the beginning of his work." In the christological debates of the fourth century, the Arians cited this verse as proof that the Logos was a creature while the Catholics maintained that it referred to the incarnate Word. Both, however, assumed that Lady Wisdom in Proverbs 8 referred to Christ.

There is uncertainty in the critical verse 30. The rare word *'amon,* rendered "master worker" by NRSV, might also mean something like "little child." (Cf. KJV's "one brought up with him.") The picture is either of Yahweh's co-worker or of a child playing in her father's workshop.

But these questions should not obscure the basic theme of Wisdom present with God in creation. The Wisdom found in the basic ordering of the world, the truth which will be enunciated in all the maxims in the following chapters of Proverbs, was involved in the origin of things. When God "drew a circle on the face of the deep," Wisdom was present. This is similar to what we mean today in saying that the natural laws which we observe today were valid in the beginning, or the Greek idea of the *logos* of the universe. While we should not uncritically amalgamate Wisdom and Word and scientific law, there are significant connections made available to Christian thought through the New Testament ideas of Christ as God's Word and Wisdom.

The final verse tells us that Wisdom also *rejoices* in the inhabited world and in humanity. There is an intrinsic joy in creation, so that scientific work is not just a grim search for facts. Beauty and pleasure in the discovery of beauty are parts of the scientific enterprise.[9] The biblical tradition allows us to see that as a share in the rejoicing of God's own Wisdom from the first moment of creation, a rejoicing which is continuous with the eschatological doxology of the universe.

PROPER 4

Psalm 96:1-9 is the RCL selection. See the discussion for Proper 24 A.

1 Kings 8:22-43 (RCL and LBW for 2 Pentecost each have shorter selections. The entire passage is preferable.)

Some elements of this prayer may go back to the dedication of Solomon's temple, but its present form reveals concerns of later generations. God would be present on Mount Zion, but Israel's later history would show that God was not restricted to any single location. The entire universe is accessible to God. Verses 27-30 here recognize the tension: God is present in the entire universe and beyond (whatever "beyond" may mean, since spatial metaphors are necessarily transcended here), but God has promised to be present in a special way in the Temple.

This tension has not disappeared in Christian thought. There is no special "holy place" for Christians, as John 4:20-24 makes clear, but the one whom "heaven and the highest heaven cannot contain" is present fully and uniquely in Jesus, and is given unreservedly to people in the Lord's Supper. The tension continues in Lutheran-Reformed differences about the presence of Christ in the Eucharist and the related christological issues. We seem to be called to new attempts to understand the relationship between God and the space-time of our universe, such as Torrance's work from a Reformed standpoint.[10]

Perhaps what we should hope for is simply a realization that this tension exists, and a sense of wonder at the idea that, however we try to make sense of it, the omnipresent God *is* present in Jesus of Nazareth. It is the sense which should be conveyed by the marvelous verse of Christina Georgina Rossetti's Christmas hymn:

> *Heaven cannot hold him,*
> *Nor earth sustain;*
> *Heaven and earth shall flee away*
> *When He comes to reign;*
> *In the bleak midwinter*
> *A stable place sufficed*
> *The Lord God Almighty,*
> *Jesus Christ.*[11]

Luke 7:1-10 (LBW for 2 Pentecost.)

It is easy to make the stories of healing in the ministry of Jesus more comprehensible by calling them "psychosomatic" and ascribing them to the profound influences which, even within the realm of "pure nature," the mind can exert on the body. The faith required for such healing is trust in healing itself, or faith in wellness. No doubt some of the healings in Scripture are of this type. (See, e.g., our discussion for Proper 25 B.) But a story like today's Gospel warns against reduction of all our Lord's cures to such effects. As the story is told, the healing takes place at a distance, and the faith which is involved is not that of the person who is healed. Perhaps more important is the fact that that faith is not of the Positive Thinking type, but a confidence in the person of Jesus. The story is difficult to fit within scientific theories of causation, but reality is not necessarily that simple.

PROPER 5

1 Kings 17:17-24; Luke 7:11-17 (LBW for 3 Pentecost.)

Here we follow up the comments made on the healing story for the previous Sunday. Today there are extreme stories of "healing," resuscitations of the dead. Explanations of "faith healing" in the usual sense are difficult because it is not easy for the dead to believe. But genuine faith in God is God's own work and gift (see Luther's explanation of the Third Article in the *Small Catechism*), and therefore has an essential relationship with the divine *creatio ex nihilo*. Thus in Romans 4 Paul connects justification of the ungodly with the resurrection of the dead, creation out of nothing, and hoping against hope.

PROPER 12

Colossians 2:6-15 [16-19] (LBW has vv. 6-15 for 10 Pentecost.)

As we reflect on the warning here against "philosophy," we should remember that the natural sciences used to be described as "natural philosophy." Two mistakes are to be avoided in such reflection: limitation of the warning to the types of gnostic mythology which the writer of Colossians had in mind, and anti-intellectualism which rejects everything outside the Bible.

The proper object of concern is the elevation of any philosophical or scientific system to a religious level. This happens when a scientific explanation, such as evolution through natural selection or behavioral psychology, is presented as an *alternative* to theological views of reality. When that happens, the energies of nature are endued with ultimate power in our lives and become modern counterparts of the "elements" (*stoicheia* — NRSV's "elemental spirits" is interpretative) of Colossians 2:8. Inordinate claims for created, penultimate entities are unmasked and defeated through the cross of Christ and returned to their proper role of creatures through whom the creator is at work.

It is not only atheists who contribute to the divinization of natural forces. Christians who think that the Bible gives scientific explanations which are competitors with, for example, evolutionary theories, may push people in the same direction. Things like "scientific creationism" are poor science and can't compete with good theories. People who are convinced by "creationists" that they have to choose between the Big Bang and Genesis 1 *as a scientific account* may well take the defenders of the faith at their word and become atheists. The warning of Matthew 18:5 is relevant here.

PROPER 13

Ecclesiastes 1:2, 12-14; 2:18-23 (LBW has 1:2; 2:18-26 for 11 Pentecost.)

A laboratory manual for a general physics course which one of us taught contained the warning: "In this *laboratory*, use the first five letters and not the last seven." In science, *labor* — whether physical, intellectual, or a combination of the two — is vital. Mere *oratory* accomplishes little. But the words of Qoholeth strike this kind of work as well as any other. Scientific work can be "vanity," emptiness, unless it is genuinely open to truth about reality. That truth may force us to abandon illusions and cherished dreams about the world, and lead to the type of skepticism which we find in Ecclesiastes.

PROPER 14

Psalm 33:12-22 (LBW has the entire Psalm for 12 Pentecost.)

This first part of the Psalm is praise to God for creation. In particular, verse 6 proclaims that all the universe is created by God's *word* — the same word, the same source of justice and order that came to the prophets. Creation "by the word of the LORD" and "by the breath of his mouth" in this verse is an example of parallelism in Hebrew poetry. In the canonical context provided by the New Testament, God's "word" and "breath" are seen as the Son and Holy Spirit.

Verses 16 and 17 should also be noted. They address the idea of security and salvation through weapons systems.

PROPER 15

Jeremiah 23:23-29 (LBW for 13 Pentecost.)

"Omnipresence" is often attributed to God by philosophical theology. Being everywhere seems a reasonable property for God to have. But on further study the idea becomes more difficult. Is *all* of God everywhere? How is the idea to be related to our scientific theories of space and time?

Jeremiah speaks here of God's presence throughout "heaven and earth," but not of God's just passively "being there." The emphasis is on the efficacy of God's *word*, the word for which the prophets are instruments. This word is more than information — it *does* things. It is irresistible (v. 29 — cf. Isaiah 55:10-11). Thus God's presence throughout the universe is pictured as an effective presence by which God's will is accomplished "in all places of his dominion" (Psalm 103:22).

This text is fundamental to the calling of the preacher, for the message which is to be proclaimed from the pulpit *is* the Word of God, the word which accomplishes all of God's work. The man or woman who receives this call should be both humbled and encouraged by that realization.

PROPER 16

Jeremiah 1:4-10 is given as an alternative by RCL. For discussion see 4 Epiphany C.

PROPER 18

Proverbs 9:8-12 is LBW's First Lesson for 16 Pentecost.

The statement of verse 10, that the fear of the LORD is the beginning of wisdom, is repeated with variations several times in Scripture (Job 28:28, Psalm 111:10, Proverbs 1:7, 9:10 and 15:33, and Sirach 1:14). Since the concept of "wisdom" comes closer than anything else in the Bible to our idea of science (though the two are certainly not identical), such a statement ought to influence our approach to the science-theology dialogue.

There is a sense in which "the fear of the LORD" is *not* necessary for science. People can be good scientists without even knowing about, let alone believing in, the God of the Bible. God has made it possible to understand the world without any reference to its creator. When Napoleon (according to the story) challenged Laplace for making no reference to God in his great work on celestial mechanics, Laplace was quite right to reply, "Sire, I did not need that hypothesis."[12]

But there are a couple of ways in which the motto of Israel's wisdom literature does apply to science. First, it is an historical fact that the type of science which actually *works* to give understanding of the physical world arose within a culture molded in fundamental ways by the Judaeo-Christian tradition. Historians of science have debated the reasons for this, and for the corresponding negative fact that science never really took off in, for example, China or Meso-America. But it does seem that, historically, the fear of the LORD (the biblical God, not simply the object of natural theology) was the beginning of science.

Secondly, an understanding of the world does not tell us what we should *do* with the knowledge and consequent power which we gain. We have enough examples of the misuse of science and technology in recent centuries to make this clear. Science does not generate an ethic for its own use. That does not mean, of course, that one must search for such an ethic in the Bible: an ethic based on "the fear of the LORD" must be presented on its own merits. But such an ethic must make use of the wisdom tradition, which culminates in Paul's picture of Christ as the crucified Wisdom of God (1 Corinthians 1:18-31). Our comments on 1 Corinthians 2 for 5 Epiphany A are relevant here.

Psalm 139:1-6, 13-18 is given as an alternative by RCL. For discussion see 3 Easter B.

PROPER 20

Amos 8:4-7 (LBW for 18 Pentecost.)

If asked to use some government official as a metaphor for God, we would probably think of a president, a judge, or a police officer. But Amos calls our attention to another figure. In one of our counties that official has the title "Sealer of Weights and Measures." That person's responsibility is to ensure that store scales, gas pumps, and so forth are accurate, so that when you pay for a gallon of gas you get a gallon, not nine-tenths of one. Amos' criticism of a measure of volume which gives the buyer less than the ephah of grain which was paid for and of a measure of weight which demands more than the shekel of silver which should be paid suggests that the prophet would have liked to have an honest "Sealer of Weights and Measures" in the Northern Kingdom.

But that is more than merely the concern of Amos. It's also *God's* concern. God cares about justice, not simply as an abstraction but as a concrete matter of ephahs and shekels.

In some cases justice can be quantified and accuracy of measurement and precision of thought are essentials for the doing of justice. Perhaps we don't often think of the Bureau of Standards as a government department concerned about justice, but in some ways it is. (Cf. also Proverbs 11:1 here.) And if this adds to our repertoire of metaphors for God, so much the better.

PROPER 23

Psalm 111 (LBW for 21 Pentecost. See the discussion for 4 Epiphany B.)

Ruth 1:1-19a; Luke 17:11-19 (The reading from Ruth is LBW's First Lesson for 21 Pentecost. RCL's selection, 2 Kings 5:1-3, 7-15c, also deals with the status of a non-Israelite, but Ruth has a more significant place in salvation history.)

Both of these texts address the issue of race, one of the major problems of our time. The Book of Ruth is not simply a romance or a story of trust in God. The writer emphasizes throughout the book that the central figure is Ruth "the Moabitess" (RSV) *(hamo'abhiyah)*, who also will be the great-grandmother of King David. In the Gospel, it is one of the despised Samaritans who is singled out for praise by Jesus.

Scientific "proofs" of the superiority of one race over another have, fortunately, fallen on hard times. It is also wrong, and unnecessary, to argue that there are no objective differences of any significance between races. Biblical inclusivity does not ignore differences, but emphasizes that God accepts people without reference to those differences. Racial diversity is part of the delight of God's creation and contributes to its health and strength.

Racial exclusiveness is a strategy by which a group's gene pool can be protected. It is not always a wise genetic strategy, for the dangers of inbreeding are well known, and it is espoused only in limited ways in Scripture. Nehemiah's policy against foreign marriages was a response to a situation in which the Jews were a small minority surrounded by hostile people, and there was a danger that the worship of Yahweh would be swamped by pagan religions if intermarriage were allowed.

But Scripture from beginning to end points away from the idea that there is a chosen biological group of humans. Finally the saints will include those "from every nation, from all tribes and peoples and languages" (Revelation 7:9). And that comes about through the great, great ... great grandson of Ruth "the Moabitess" (Matthew 1:5).

PROPER 24

Psalm 121 (LBW for 22 Pentecost.)

We have a lot of problems today but, except for the tides and the possibility of skin cancer, the malign influences of the heavenly bodies which the psalmist spoke of (v. 6) are not among them. The demythologizing of the universe, which is a proper part of Christianity, and the development of science both have helped to free people from such fears. The popularity of some New Age thought, and especially of astrology, threatens to return people to that ancient bondage. Warnings about pagan world views which would have seemed hopelessly outdated from the pulpits of fifty years ago may have to be dusted off by today's preachers.

PROPER 25

Psalm 65 is given as an alternative by RCL. For discussion see Harvest in the section of texts common for each year.

PROPER 27

Luke 20:27-38 (LBW for 25 Pentecost.)

Belief in an afterlife on the basis of something intrinsic to human nature is common in many cultures and religions. The idea of immortality of the soul is a good expample. Israel's thought was different in this regard. There was quite early the concept of a shadowy kind of half-existence in Sheol, but explicit statements about resurrection of the dead are found only in late texts of the Old Testament, Isaiah 26:19 and Daniel 12:3. Thus the conservative Sadducees did not accept the idea.

Jesus uses a "proof text" whose relevance is not obvious to the modern exegete, but the passage about the burning bush is from the Torah, and therefore authoritative for the Sadducees. From the standpoint of the New Testament, it is a statement about the resurrection *because Jesus interprets it that way.* There is a "backward in time" aspect to the interpretation of the Exodus text which means that it cannot be fully understood only in its setting in the Hebrew Scriptures. (Cf. Luke 24:25-27.) The idea that actions can occur "backward in time," that effects can *precede* their causes, has been used most prominently in science fiction, but it has also been taken seriously by physicists.[13]

Jesus describes the continued existence of those who have died by saying that they are all alive *to God.* It is because of God that life does not end with death. This need not (though it could) be interpreted in terms of a continued existence of souls or spirits of the dead in our present. If we picture God as in some sense outside our time, our future resurrection is in God's present. The emphasis here is on a continued relationship between each person and God rather than on an intrinsic human immortality. Even the text in the Apocrypha which speaks of immortality of the soul points in that direction: "The souls of the just are in God's hand" (Wisdom 3:1 NEB).

Psalm 98 is given as an alternative by RCL both for this Sunday and the next. See the note for 6 Easter B.

CHRIST THE KING

Colossians 1:11-20 (LBW begins with v. 13.)

The biblical text which is authoritative is that which stands in Scripture now. It is important to try to discern the various sources and redactions which lie behind the canonical text, but the final concern of those who are to preach these texts is with their present form. Verses 15-20 of this passage from Colossians may be based on a pre-Christian hymn in which the specifically Christian phrases *tes ekklesias* (v. 18) and *eirenopoiesas dia tou haimatos tou staurou autou* (v. 20) were inserted.[14] The canonical text then speaks of a cosmic role of the crucified Christ who is the head of the Church.

Christ's activity is past, present, and future. All things were created in him and through him. He is "before all things" and was the agent of creation in the beginning. He is the agent of the ongoing maintenance and preservation of the world: "In him all things hold together." And all things were created "for him": the universe finds its fulfillment in him.

It has often been argued that Copernicus began a process of removing humanity from a central place in the world. In some ways that is an exaggeration: in the medieval view, the earth (with Hell at its core) was the *bottom* as well as the center of the universe, and heaven was more important than earth. The theory of evolution through natural selection played a larger role in removing humanity from a central position, for it seemed to say that our species came to be only through a chance assortment of random circumstances.

In recent years, the controversial "anthropic principles" of modern cosmology have moved in the opposite direction, suggesting that the development of intelligent life is a critical feature of the cosmos. (See our discussions for Proper 10 B and Trinity C.) Perhaps the universe could not even exist if such life did not develop within it. These ideas remain speculative even within science. They cannot prove that Christianity is true, nor can Christian theology prove the anthropic principles as a matter of science. But Christian thought provides a strong *parallel* to anthropic principles. The picture in the Christ Hymn of Colossians is of the universe *(ta panta)* reaching its goal, not simply in humanity as such but in humanity indwelt by God in Jesus Christ. This can be referred to as a *the*anthropic principle. What makes the universe possible, what holds it together and is its final purpose, is Jesus Christ.[15]

And it is the *crucified* Christ who is all that. It is "by the blood of his cross" that "all things" are reconciled to their creator and are brought to the purpose God intends for them. If there is a theological "Copernican revolution," it involves the radical belief that "all things" are centered on the crucified Son of God. (See the discussion of 1 Corinthians 1:18-31 for 4 Epiphany A.)

"All things" must include any extraterrestrial beings. Scientists are divided over whether or not intelligent life is to be expected anywhere else in the universe, and people tend also to be divided in their instinctive reactions to such an idea. Some who have dismissed the idea of God may cling with religious fervor to belief in ETs to mitigate cosmic loneliness. Others are wary about the prospect of alien visitors. Americans, remembering the history of the conquest of their continent, may be ambivalent about the possibility.

What would be our religious response if ETs visited us, or if we were to encounter them in our explorations of space? The preacher does not have to speculate on the scientific probability for life elsewhere in the universe, but this Sunday might be an opportunity for a story sermon using science fiction motifs to bring out some of the cosmic significance of the Colossians text.

DAY OF THANKSGIVING

Deuteronomy 26:1-11 (See the commentary for 1 Lent C.)

Endnotes

1. John A.T. Robinson, *The Body* (Westminster, Philadelphia, 1977), p. 58.
2. Pierre Teilhard de Chardin, *Activation of Energy* (Harcourt Brace Jovanovich, New York, 1970), pp. 115-116.

3. Dante, *The Divine Comedy,* "Paradise," canto 14, line 43.

4. Dirk J. Struik, *A Concise History of Mathematics,* 2nd revised ed. (Dover, New York, 1948), p. 165.

5. For an interesting fictional use of the latter see Madeleine L'Engle, *A Wrinkle in Time* (Dell, New York, 1962).

6. G.B. Caird, *The Revelation of St. John the Divine* (Harper & Row, New York, 1966), pp. 279-280.

7. C.S. Lewis, *That Hideous Strength* (Macmillan, New York, 1946).

8. Barrow and Tipler, *The Anthropic Cosmological Principle.*

9. S. Chandrasekhar, "Beauty and the Quest for Beauty in Science," *Physics Today 32,* July 1979, p. 25.

10. Thomas F. Torrance, *Space, Time and Incarnation* (Oxford, London, 1969).

11. Christina Georgina Rossetti, "In the bleak mid-winter," Hymn #36 in *Service Book and Hymnal* (Augsburg, Minneapolis, 1958), Verse 2.

12. Kaiser, *Creation and the History of Science,* p. 267.

13. Nahin, *Time Machines.*

14. For detailed discussion of the passage with numerous references see Eduard Lohse, *Colossians and Philemon* (Fortress, Philadelphia, 1971), pp. 32-61.

15. George L. Murphy, "The Incarnation as a Theanthropic Principle," *Word & World XIII,* p. 256, 1993.

Texts Common To Each Year

THE NATIVITY OF OUR LORD

Psalms 96, 97, 98

The Psalms for all three Christmas services celebrate the kingship of Yahweh. At Christmas they are seen in a new light. They celebrate God's rule not as an outsider but as the one "born to be king" and sharing in the life of creation. Some of the comments on Psalm 96 for Proper 24 A are applicable to the other Psalms for the Nativity of our Lord as well.

CHRISTMAS EVE (I) and CHRISTMAS DAWN (II)

Isaiah 9:2-7

The royal titles given here to the coming child were seen, in the time of Isaiah and at that of Jesus' birth, over against the claims of the political empires of Assyria and Rome. Today and in the twenty-first century the birth of the Messiah must be proclaimed in a context of economic and technological imperiums which determine the disposition of earth's resources and the energies which science makes available. Faithful preaching at Christmas on this text will present Jesus as the alternative power for the powerless, and his birth as the coming of the one who has the authority to redistribute wealth, reorder care of the earth, and revise priorities for the use of its resources.

Luke 2:1-20 (RCL gives 2:1-14 [15-20] for Christmas Eve and 2:[1-7] 8-20 for Christmas Dawn. Here we reflect especially on vv. 8-14.)

Mention of "the heavenly host" is double-valued. It refers to the angelic armies, but still carries the ancient idea of the stars of heaven as well. In a way, the angelic host in Luke's Christmas story parallels the Star of Bethlehem in Matthew's. The heavenly bodies and the entire universe join in celebrating the birth of their king.

The birth of Jesus at Christmas is the fulfillment of the promise that the creator who made the world out of nothing in the beginning has power to cause Immanuel, God with us, to be conceived in the empty womb of a girl newly become a woman. That empty womb becomes the nothingness out of which God will call the whole new creation.

CHRISTMAS DAY (III)

Hebrews 1:1-4 [5-12] (LBW has vv. 1-9.)

The words from verse 3, "Upholding the universe by his word of power" (RSV), are used as a motto by the American Scientific Affiliation, an organization of Christians in various areas of scientific work. The Christian understanding of the world is much more profound than a general theistic belief that "God" made the world. Jesus Christ, God's full and final revelation (v. 1), is the One through whom God "created the worlds" and keeps the universe in being. Christmas is not a time when most people would expect to hear about creation, but perhaps they can use a surprise, a cosmic surprise stated very well by Karl Barth:

> *The world came into being, it was created and sustained by the little child that was born at Bethlehem, by the man who died on the cross of Golgotha, and the third day rose again.* That *is the Word of creation, by which all things were brought into being. That is where the* meaning *of creation comes from, and that is why it says at the beginning of the Bible: "In the beginning God made heaven and earth and God said, Let there be . . . ."*[1]

John 1:1-14

To speak of Christ, the author of the Fourth Gospel used a term which at that time was broad and transcultural, and which today has the potential for significant contact with themes of the science-theology dialogue. "Word," the Greek *logos*, has its origin in the "word of the LORD," *dabhar YHWH*, which came to the prophets, a weighty and active divine expression (Amos 8:11-12; Jeremiah 23:29). It is the Word through which God created the universe: the echoes of Genesis 1 in the prologue of John's gospel are unmistakable. (The *memra* or "utterance" of the targums may be the link between the older biblical usage and that in John, as the connection between the targum on Numbers and John 3:14 suggests.[2]) But the Johannine *logos* also connects up with the use of the term in Greek philosophy, a use which has connotations of both "word" and "reason." Thus God's self-expression ("At the beginning God expressed himself" is J.B. Phillips' paraphrase of v. 1a) and the divine rationality are encompassed. While philosophical concepts like the World Reason of the Stoics do not lie behind the prologue, John makes it possible for christology to make contact with such ideas.

Christ as *logos* is thus the source of the world's pattern. That does not mean that he is something like the laws of nature, for that would suggest a basically passive and impersonal role. The laws of nature are *contingent* — they could have been different, and they are as they are because God so chooses. But the Word is the source and maintenance of the world's rationality.

Augustine said that he had found "In the beginning was the Word" in Plato, but that he had never read there that "the Word became flesh." The source of the universe's rationality has chosen to be united personally with the universe. In the modern description of elementary particles by quantum field theory, the basic laws of physics which describe the interactions of matter are indissolubly united with the substance of the world. This can provide an analogy for the Incarnation of the Word which is perhaps more helpful today than older images like the union of "fire" and "iron" in glowing iron.

The Word has come to "dwell" among us (v. 14). The destiny of the universe is the embodied Word, a theme which parallels the anthropic principles of modern cosmology which speak of a central role for intelligent life in the universe. (See the discussion of Colossians 1:13-20 for Christ the King C.)

2 CHRISTMAS

Sirach [Ecclesiasticus] 24:1-12 is suggested as an alternate First Lesson by RCL. This speech of Holy Wisdom provides some of the biblical background for the *logos* concept of the Fourth Gospel.

Ephesians 1:3-14 (LBW has 1:3-6, 15-18. See the discussion for Proper 10 B.)

John 1:[1-9] 10-18 (See the discussion of vv. 1-14 for Christmas Day.)

EPIPHANY

Ephesians 3:1-12 (LBW has vv. 2-12.)

This festival celebrates the revelation of Christ to the nations, and thus throughout the world. Ephesians tells us that God's plan does not even end with the proclamation of the gospel in all the earth. The Church has an even greater mission, to proclaim God's wisdom "in the heavenly places" (v. 10).

We think first of Christ's ascension in that connection, as Ephesians 1:19-23 (discussed for Ascension Day) suggests. But the proclamation of the gospel on earth takes place through human witnesses, and perhaps its announcement in the heavenly places does as well. We don't usually think of space exploration as having much to do with evangelism, and we should be careful about making such a connection in simplistic ways. But we also should not be too shy of some imaginative thought along that line. In a time when science fiction films and television series like *Star Trek* are very popular, a preacher might want to develop a science fiction story sermon to address texts like this one.

Matthew 2:1-12

The magi were the scholars of ancient Persia, trained in the Zoroastrian religious tradition, in astrology and other mystical ideas of the time, and in the natural sciences of the period. Persian ideas influenced the later writings of the Old Testament and the intertestamental period. Ignatius of Antioch saw the coming of the magi as a submission of the powers of magic and the demons to the rule of Christ.[3] That analysis may have been too optimistic: astrology was taken seriously by educated people for another sixteen hundred years after the magi were led by the star, and the resurgence of it and other forms of pseudo-science in the New Age movement shows that it still retains some power. But it still does not *work*. Christianity (as long as it isn't tempted to try to be simply a newer and better magic) should stand firmly with real science against the cheap imitation sciences of popular culture.

Astrology has no scientific basis, but it is still a big business. People pay good money to call 900 numbers and get advice from a "psychic astrologer." Preachers need to be aware that they may have people in their congregations who engage in this and other New Age practices and see no tension between them and Christianity. As with all deeply-held beliefs, acceptance of astrology should be approached with care and sensitivity, but it should not be ignored.

And in view of this, how astonishing it is that God meets the magi within their own understanding, employing a vision which makes sense within their limited view of the world to lead them to the Christ child! What has this to say about bridging gaps between religion and science/technology?

Seeking help from human power and authority on their quest, the magi stir up opposition that threatens the life of the infant Immanuel. What parallels to this story of the consultation with Herod are evoked as we seek a vision for the best uses for science and technology? What opposition from the powerful is stirred to prevent implementation or co-opt it so that it poses no threat to those in control?

ASH WEDNESDAY

2 Corinthians 5:20b—6:10 (LBW ends with 6:2.)

Greek has two words for time. *Chronos* is approximately our everyday concept, a measure of duration. *Kairos*, on the other hand, is time as an occasion, giving a sense of the *quality* of time. The "day of salvation," when there is the opportunity to respond to God's offer, differs from other days. Our digital watches, molecular clocks, and measurements of astronomical movements determine *chronos* but are blind to *kairos*.

God's saving work does not abolish time. In fact, the Incarnation is God's choice to participate fully in the space-time relationships of our world. And because of the Incarnation, time is made salvific. Its saving quality is not restricted to our past, but is shared by the moments when the risen Christ is encountered in proclamation, when people are baptized into the death and resurrection of Jesus, and by his *anamnesis* in the Supper. It is "the acceptable time" as long as God leaves the offer open. (See also Hebrews 4 here.)

The church year is not an essential part of Christianity, but it can be very useful. If nothing else, it can illustrate the concepts of *chronos* and *kairos*. The secular calendar helps us to keep track of intervals of time. That is not the main purpose of the church's calendar. That is a representation of

God's *kairoi,* a way of keeping in touch with unique times of salvation history. Now, whatever the world may be doing this February or March, it is Ash Wednesday. It is time to remember that we are dust, time to start on the way to the desert with the Lord, time again to take with renewed seriousness his call to be disciples. The acceptable time may come in July or November too, but we emphasize that *kairos* liturgically today.

There is a common experience in our technological world which can illustrate the distinction between the two ideas of time. As you sit in an airport waiting area, you hear departures of different flights being announced. For you, most of them simply correspond to different entries in a timetable. But when the departure of *your* flight comes over the PA system, that is the *kairos* for you. It's time to get on board or be left behind.

SUNDAY OF THE PASSION

Philippians 2:5-11

When the full passion narrative is read on this day, there may be little appetite for a lengthy sermon. But this text, which speaks of the *kenosis,* the emptying, of the Son of God, of his death, and of cosmic obeisance to the exalted crucified One, can keep our understanding of the effects of his passion from being too limited. Every creature in the universe will worship him, and this will mean the ordering of all nature in justice and peace.

TUESDAY IN HOLY WEEK

John 12:20-36 (See the discussion for 5 Lent B.)

WEDNESDAY IN HOLY WEEK

Romans 5:6-11 is LBW's Second Lesson. See the discussion for Proper 6 A.

EASTER VIGIL

The Song of the Three Jews 35-65.

The proclamation of the Word for the vigil comes with a number of rather lengthy readings, and a sermon, if any, will probably be brief. A number of the Old Testament readings focus on creation (e.g., Genesis 1:1—3:24 or the shorter alternative 1:1—2:2) or provide anticipations of the supreme act of new creation in the resurrection of Jesus (e.g., Ezekiel 37:1-14).[4] The story of the Flood, concluding with God's covenant with all living things, is especially noteworthy for our concerns. (See the discussion for 1 Lent B.)

The canticle *Benedicite, Omnia Opera (Lutheran Book of Worship* Canticle #18), a selection from The Canticle of Azariah and the Song of the Three Jews in the Apocrypha, is the response to the final reading from Daniel 3. It is a wonderful praise of God by the whole creation, sung out of the fire of persecution. This expands upon the theme of Psalm 148 (upon which we comment for 1 Christmas A), and in fact can be thought of as a biblical commentary on that Psalm.

The universe is God's, and though the world may destroy God's faithful people, God remembers and vindicates them. Therefore God's people can have courage to persevere in their covenant responsibilities of caring for the earth and of voicing creation's worship of God.

Exodus 15:1-11, part of the response to the fourth reading, is discussed for Easter C, where it is LBW's First Lesson.

EASTER EVENING

Isaiah 25:6-9 (See the discussion for Proper 23 A.)

ASCENSION DAY

Acts 1:1-11; Ephesians 1:15-23 (LBW begins with v. 16.)

Today we celebrate both the ascension of Christ and his "session" at the right hand of the Father. The First Lesson may suggest an incredible pre-scientific picture of Jesus rising a few miles above the clouds and sitting on a throne in the sky. The Second Lesson says that "God ... seated him at his right hand in the heavenly places" (v. 20). But Christ is also the One "who fills all in all" (v. 23). The picture in Ephesians is not of Jesus localized in heaven, but of him as the cosmic ruler who is immediately present to the entire universe. God's "right hand" is not a single place but the power with which God rules, so that Luther said simply that the right hand of God is everywhere.

In order to make sense of this message in relation to scientific views of the universe, remember that modern science has already moved well beyond common sense ideas of space and time. Einstein's relativity theories have made us realize that the real geometry of the universe has to be determined from experience, and not from an analysis of what is supposed to be intrinsic to our thought about the world, as Kant believed. Space-time is inextricably linked with the material of the world and its behavior. And the Christian claim is that the cross, resurrection, and ascension of Jesus make up the most fundamental happening in the history of the universe.

VIGIL OF PENTECOST

Romans 8:14-17, 22-27 (See the discussion for Proper 11 A.)

SAINT ANDREW

Psalm 19:1-6 (See the discussion for 3 Lent B.)

SAINT JOHN

Genesis 1:1-5, 26-31 (See the discussion for Trinity A.)

THE NAME OF JESUS

Psalm 8 (See the discussion for Trinity C.)

SAINT MARK

Psalm 57

The superscription calls this a psalm of David "when he fled from Saul, in the cave." It is thus typologically a Psalm of the resurrection of Christ. Verse 8 invites us to think of the moment of Christ's resurrection as an awakening, and the refrain in verses 6 and 11 invites us to see that as the awakening of the whole creation.

NATIVITY OF SAINT JOHN THE BAPTIST

Malachi 3:1-4 (See the discussion for 2 Advent C.)

SAINT BARTHOLOMEW

1 Corinthians 12:27-31a (See the discussion for 3 Epiphany C.)

John 1:43-51

In Genesis 28:12, in the story of Jacob's dream at Bethel, it is possible to see the angels ascending and descending on *Jacob*. (Grammatically, *bo* could be "on him" as well as "on it.") Some of the rabbis did read the passage in this way, and saw Israel as the bridge between earth and heaven. In John 1:51 it is not Israel's ancestor but its "King" who is that bridge. The connection between God and God's creation is the incarnate Word.

HOLY CROSS DAY

Psalm 98 (See the discussion for Christmas.)

Isaiah 45:21-25 is LBW's First Lesson for this festival.

Every knee shall bow to the God of Israel (v. 23), a thought which is transferred to Christ in Philippians 2:11. (See the discussion for Passion Sunday.) In a trinitarian understanding, there is no substantial difference. If every knee bows to God, then every shred of knowledge shall be used at God's command and every exercise of power consider God's will. The ethic which gives priority to justice to the neighbor and praise to God "the Almighty" is valid wherever in the universe we might travel, in whatever kind of work we may be employed. Bowing the knee to God is not a matter of proper court ritual but is to happen in each word we speak and each deed we do. Those of us engaged in science, engineering, and medicine are to see those activities also as part of our homage.

1 Corinthians 1:18-24 (See the discussion for 4 Epiphany A.)

John 12:20-33 (See the discussion for 5 Lent B.)

COMMEMORATION OF SAINTS

1 Corinthians 1:26-31 (See the discussion for 4 Epiphany A.)

COMMEMORATION OF THEOLOGIANS

Wisdom 7:7-14

The work of the theologian differs from that of the scientist because their "texts" are different. The theologian reads Scripture while the natural scientist reads the world. (The idea of the cosmos as *sefer*, text, goes back to medieval Jewish thinkers, and the concept of Scripture and nature as God's "two books" was used by, for example, Galileo.) This does not mean that there is no commonality between theology and natural science, for the "author" of both books is the triune God. One way of expressing this commonality is in terms of the Wisdom which is the subject of the book by that name in the Apocrypha. The world was created in God's wisdom (Psalm 104:24), which is the secret of creation.[5] This Wisdom could be understood by Jews in the intertestamental period as something to be found in Torah (Sirach 24, Baruch 3:9-37), and by early Christians as incarnate in Jesus. (See 1 Corinthians 1:18-31 and the *chiasmus* of Matthew 11:2 and 19.) Thus one answer to the question, "What do scientists and theologians have in common?" is "The study of Wisdom."

1 Corinthians 2:6-10, 13-16 (See the discussion for 5 Epiphany A.)

Matthew 13:47-52 (See the discussion for Proper 12 A.)

COMMEMORATION OF ARTISTS AND SCIENTISTS

Psalm 96 (See the discussion for Proper 24 A.)

Matthew 13:44-52 (See the discussion for Proper 12 A.)

Christians commemorated in the Church's calendar have usually been those notable for some specifically "religious" reason. It is right that we remember and honor apostles and evangelists, martyrs and missionaries, pastors and theologians. But "church work" does not exhaust the list of avenues of service to which God calls us. Since many people have the idea that there is some incompatibility between Christianity and science, it can be helpful to call attention to Christians whose vocation has been science, engineering, or medicine. The

Lutheran Book of Worship lists commemorations of the scientists Nicolaus Copernicus and Leonhard Euler for 24 May, and the nurses Florence Nightingale and Clara Maass on 13 August, and the *Book of Common Prayer* commemorates the medieval scientist Robert Grosseteste on 9 October. The traditional festival of Saint Luke the physician on 18 October might also be noted. Other commemorations — for example, of Louis Pasteur or James Clerk Maxwell — would also be appropriate. Some attention to the lives of such Christians would help to bring out the possibility of consonance between Christianity and science. (Clara Maass died as a volunteer for experiments to determine the cause and cure for yellow fever in 1901. There can be an element of martyrdom involved in scientific work.)

DEDICATION AND ANNIVERSARY

1 Kings 8:22-30 (See the discussion for Proper 4 C.)

HARVEST

Psalm 65

This speaks vividly of God's maintenance of the world, and of harvest as the gift of *God.* God "visits" the earth and waters it (v. 9). The grain is "prepared" (v. 10), almost as if we were to picture God working on each individual stalk. But of course Israel, though not having a concept of an independent natural order, recognized the regularities of the processes which bring the harvest. And we can understand those processes, from the nuclear reactions at the sun's core which provide solar energy through weather to the botanical processes by which the grain ripens, in scientific terms. We don't *have* to say anything about God's involvement in the process, but faith in God as creator will lead us to do so.

This was formalized in traditional doctrines of providence as *concurrence,* the idea that in everything that happens in the world God is at work through natural processes. We look ultimately to God to provide for us because God is also the creator of those natural processes and the laws which govern them. (Those laws are *contingent:* they might have been different had God so chosen.) Our scientific comprehension of the bounty of harvest does not give us less cause to thank God than Israel had. If anything, we have *more* to be grateful for because we can thank God for the rationality of nature.

Deuteronomy 26:1-11 (See the discussion for 1 Lent C.)

NATIONAL HOLIDAY

Psalm 20

This forms with Psalm 21 a pair of royal Psalms. Psalm 20 is the king before battle, and Psalm 21 is a thanksgiving after victory. They are not pacifist hymns: the nation is going to fight, and asks God for aid. Yet a clear distinction is maintained between going to war and trusting in one's own military might. Verses 7-8 here reject confidence in horses and chariots, the state-of-the-art weapons systems of the nations, as idolatry which will lead to failure.

Much of the Christian tradition has spoken of a possibility of "just war" (perhaps "justifiable war" is better), an idea different from either pacifism or "holy war." War may, in some situations, be a regrettable necessity. In no situation, however, are we to put our final trust in military might. This warning needs to be heard today when science-based technology gives us weapons and defenses which so easily give the illusion of supreme security. But the only ultimate security, in war or peace, is to "call upon the name of the LORD our God."

PEACE

Micah 4:1-5

Verses 1-3 duplicate Isaiah 2:2-4, which is assigned for 1 Advent A. (The discussion there gives a general explication of technological themes raised by Isaiah 2.) The beating of swords into plowshares has been taken as a profound symbol of the hope for peace, as in the statue which stands outside the United Nations building in New York. It is sometimes forgotten that this hope is not unambiguous within the canon: Joel 3:10 calls for plowshares to be beaten into swords and pruning hooks into spears. A straightforward proof-texting approach cannot settle the war-peace question in any given situation, though the fact that "swords into plowshares" outnumbers "plowshares into swords" two to one in the Bible may be significant!

In the just war tradition, one of the criteria for going to war is that the goal of the war must be peace. *Shalom* is the eschatological goal, but in our time before the eschaton, war may be the more appropriate choice in some circumstances and peace in others. The imagery used by the prophets points out that the same technology can be used for either peace or war. The same metallurgy can be used for plowshares or swords. The effects of technology, and the question of its morality, depend on the human wills which choose how that technology will be used.

STEWARDSHIP OF CREATION

Psalm 104:1, 13-24 *or* **25-37** (See the discussion for Pentecost A.)

Job 39:1-11, 16-18

The physicist Victor Weisskopf wrote a popular book about the scientific understanding of the world titled *Knowledge and Wonder*.[6] "Knowledge" is usually emphasized when we talk about science as an objective compilation of facts and their relationships. A science that didn't give us real knowledge of the world wouldn't be worth much. But "wonder" is also important if one is to be a really good scientist, or even if one is simply to appreciate science. Those who don't believe in

God as the creator experience this wonder, as British cosmologist Fred Hoyle's statement about the fineness of the universe "in concept and design" shows. In the closing chapters of Job, God appeals to this sense of wonder and says, "I'm behind it." The world is wonderful because God made and makes it so. As stewards of creation, part of our calling is to have such a sense of wonder and to help preserve the marvels of creation.

NEW YEAR'S EVE

Psalm 102:24-28

The decades of life or the centuries of history can present a depressing vista because we are aware of the shortness of our lives, and especially of the healthy and useful parts of our lives. This is exacerbated for us today, with our knowledge that the universe has been in existence for ten or fifteen billion years, and the earth for about four and a half billion. Even the whole history of the human race has covered only a small fraction of the age of the earth. (If the age of the earth is taken as one day, humanity would be in existence for a fraction of a minute before midnight.) It is all the more important for us to remember the psalmist's confidence that God endures.

Endnotes

1. Karl Barth, *Dogmatics in Outline* (Harper & Row, New York, 1959), p. 58.

2. Raymond E. Brown, *The Gospel According to John (i-xii)*, The Anchor Bible 29 (Doubleday, Garden City NY, 1966), Appendix II and p. 133.

3. "The Epistle of Ignatius to the Ephesians" in *The Ante-Nicene Fathers,* Vol. I, (Wm. B. Eerdmans, Grand Rapids MI, 1979), Ch. XIX, p. 57.

4. A chart showing the vigil readings in several different rites is on pp. 80-81 of Gabe Huck and Mary Ann Simcoe (ed.), *Triduum Sourcebook* (Liturgy Training Publications, Chicago, 1983).

5. von Rad, *Wisdom in Israel,* Chapter 9.

6. Victor F. Weisskopf, *Knowledge and Wonder,* revised ed. (Doubleday, Garden City, NY, 1966).

Free Texts

Exodus 31:1-11

The phrase "spiritual gifts" usually suggests qualities or abilities which are thought of as peculiarly "religious." Paul lists such gifts of the Spirit in Romans 12:6-8 and 1 Corinthians 12:4-10. The passage in Exodus 31 is likely to come as a surprise. Preparations are being made to construct the tent of meeting and its furnishings and to make vestments for the priests, and God tells Moses that people have been given "divine spirit" (*ruach 'elohim*; the alternate translation, "the spirit of God," is given in the NRSV margin) in order to carry out this work. Carpentry, metalworking, and sewing can be spiritual gifts.

One might go on to speak of the inspiration of all technology. The subject in this text, however, is not technology in general but technology within the community of God's people, serving God's purpose. While all technology depends in a fundamental way upon God, technology directed to wrong ends is, in Pauline terms, "flesh" rather than "spirit." Technology in the proper relationship with God's purpose, on the other hand, is properly "spiritual."

Much the same can be said of the gifts in Paul's lists. Teaching and even "speaking in tongues" are done by people outside the community of God's people, and may serve evil purposes. It is when they are in line with God's intention for the world that they are gifts of the Spirit.

Christians who work in the sciences or engineering have sometimes been made to think that they should leave this aspect of their lives at the church door. If their community of faith has shown no real hostility to their work (and this has happened), it may also have shown little appreciation for it. Attitudes may be changed if some attention is given to the possibility of scientific and technological abilities being gifts of the Spirit.

Leviticus 25:1-24

This would be a good text for "Stewardship of Creation Sunday" or any time when a scriptural word about care of the earth is needed. If parishioners wonder why churches are concerning themselves with environmental matters, the answer here is simply because the Bible tells them to! The Israelites are told, as part of God's covenant with them, that they are to let their land lie fallow at regular intervals. This is an elementary practical way to try to preserve and restore fertility. Today's farmers will look to science to help determine the best patterns of crop rotation and other ways of caring for the land. The point which our text makes for us is not so much the precise method given in Leviticus but the fact that care for the earth is a clear *religious* concern, part of obedient service to the God of the covenant. This is not so surprising if we remember that God's covenant is not just with Israel, or even the human race, but with "all flesh that is on the earth" (Genesis 9:8-17; see also Hosea 2:18). Furthermore, the "new covenant" in the blood of Christ is established under the forms of the bread and wine which come from the earth (1 Corinthians 11:24-25).

We see here also that care for the earth is closely tied to justice for people. Racial and ethnic minorities and the poor today often suffer the most from damage to the environment; it is easier to dispose of toxic wastes in their neighborhoods than in those of the well-to-do. (This is the problem sometimes referred to as "environmental racism.")

Justice also requires that the burden of solutions to environmental problems be distributed equitably. All of us will have to pay some price for protection of the environment, but people who get their living from the land or waters should not have to pay a disproportionate share. God's covenant commits us to justice for the earth *and* for all humanity.

Job 28:20-28

This passage is part of an interlude within Job's self-defense against God. The question of where wisdom is to be found is central to the drama of the story of Job, for Job believes that God unfairly hides wisdom and knowledge from humanity (vv. 20-21). But the finale of the story is foreshadowed in v. 28.

> *And [God] said to humankind,*
> *"Truly, the fear of the Lord, that is wisdom;*
> *and to depart from evil is understanding."*

Here Job implies that this is a weak out for God. God, he says, needs no self-defense, only threats. But, as God claims in Chapters 38 and 39, and as Job finally realizes in Chapter 42, it is indeed wise to be in awe of God, for we cannot know everything. (See commentary for Proper 7 B.) Human beings are *finite* creatures. We cannot experience the depth of reality that God experiences. Thus one moral of the story of Job, captured in this foreshadowing of the end, is that human knowledge and wisdom (understanding) are *limited*.

There may be a hint of a theology of the cross in verse 22. "Abaddon and Death," the limits of our earthly experience, have heard a "rumor" of genuine wisdom.

Isaiah 2:6-22

We discussed the opening verses of this chapter and the idea of appropriate technology for 1 Advent A. The rest of the chapter suggests two other themes related to technology.

Science, Technology and Idolatry: In verse 8 the prophet speaks of the fashioning and worship of idols. Often we think of these as images of gods, but humans "bow down" to things they have made which are not explicitly religious. How often we find ourselves worshipping the products of our technology, seeking security and fulfillment in the "work of our hands"! When faced with intractable social or environmental problems we seek a technological fix. Many people place their ultimate hopes on medical science and technology. Some seek to "play god" with life-span increasing technologies or genetic manipulation.

This is not to say that people of faith should abandon science and technology. The theme of appropriate technology provides a positive role for technology and science. As we struggle to understand the possibilities and problems of genetic manipulation, even the science and technology embodied in this form of human activity might have redemptive power.[1] But we must consider the ways in which we have replaced faith in God with faith in science and/or technology. To what degree has science become our god? To what extent have we bowed down to technological imperatives instead of those of our faith?

Technology and Hubris: The whole of Isaiah 2 provides a third entree into issues of technology and faith. This is the link between sinful human pride — *hubris* — and technology.

The NRSV gives verses 5-22 the heading, "Judgment Pronounced on Arrogance." The prophet describes the pride of the House of Jacob and God's response "in the days to come." We catch glimpses of technology: "There is no end to their chariots" (v. 7), and the LORD will be "against every high tower, and against every fortified wall; against all the ships of Tarshish, and against all the beautiful craft" (vv. 12, 15-16). Again the judgment is against not merely weapons, but any technology which embodies *hubris*. This theme is forcefully expressed in the story of the Tower of Babel: See the commentary for Pentecost C.

Sirach [Ecclesiasticus] 38:1-15

These verses from the Apocrypha are the most sustained discussion of physicians and medicine in the Bible and give quite a positive view of the healing art. Physicians are worthy of honor because God has created them for healing (v. 1). Medicines too are God's creation, things that God has arranged for the earth to produce, and it is foolish to despise them (v. 4). The example which the writer gives in v. 5, Moses' use of a piece of wood to sweeten the bitter waters of Marah (Exodus 15:22-25), is not an appeal to miracle but precisely an illustration of the kind of healing powers available in creation.

Sirach does not neglect the role of prayer in healing, but observes the proper order. First one is to pray (v. 9), and then consult the physician (v. 12). Compare here our discussion of Mark 6:1-13 and the anointing of the sick for Proper 9 B. This text from Sirach would be a helpful reading for a service of healing. It would help to bring out the fact that prayers for healing are not intended to *replace* the work of the healing arts and sciences. We are called to thank God for those arts and sciences, and for the men and women who practice them.[2]

Comparison of the Greek and Hebrew versions of the last verse produces some ambiguity. (For a long time, Sirach was known only in Greek. Parts of a Hebrew version were found a century ago, but it is not clear which comes closest to the original.[3]) The Hebrew maintains the note of respect for doctors ("He who sins against his Maker, will be defiant toward the physician"), but the Greek (". . . may he fall into the hands of the physician") gives a negative view. The latter idea may have to do with the belief that illness is a punishment for sin. And it is true that some sick people are like the woman who "had endured much under many physicians, and had spent all that she had; and she was no better, but rather grew worse" (Mark 5:26). Doctors are not perfect, and medicine today still involves art as well as science.

The verses about doctors and medicine are part of a discussion in Chapter 38 of various honorable callings, those of scholars, workers in crafts, and smiths. These are all good and they maintain the fabric of this world (38:34 NEB), but Sirach gives them all second place to the study of God's law (39:1-11).

Wisdom 7:7-22

Verses 7-14 of this passage have been discussed for the Commemoration of Theologians. The remaining verses speak of some of the things which God's Wisdom enables a person to understand; these are things which today are considered parts of physics, astronomy, zoology, botany, meteorology, psychology, and medicine.

Knowledge of these fields is not the highest wisdom of God. What is most important in Israel's wisdom literature is to know God and God's will. But the fact that "a knowledge of the structure of the world and the operation of the elements" (v. 17 NEB) is a gift of God is not insignificant. If the created world is indeed good, then understanding of it and the way it works is desirable. The ancient wisdom traditions in which Israel shared were not concerned only with abstract philosophy, but with that which enabled people to deal wisely with the world and with human society.

Today that view of wisdom will encompass science and technology. And it will go beyond a "how" understanding — how natural systems function and how to do things — to provide ethical guidance for the use of science and technology. The present passage is set within a whole book in which the Wisdom of God is presented as a guide for all of life.

1 Timothy 6:20-21

A brief warning in connection with these verses is in order because the King James Version can be misleading at this point. It speaks at the end of v. 20 of "oppositions of science falsely so called." Christians upset about scientific developments, such as evolutionary theories, have cited these verses to show that the Bible warns against false science. But *gnoseos* (NRSV "knowledge") in this context does not mean "science" in the modern sense. It refers rather to the elaborate philosophical and religious systems of Gnosticism which were strong rivals of Christianity during the early centuries of the Church.[4]

There is, of course, false science, and scientific developments are sometimes used to attack Christianity. Today science has been successful in so many ways that people may be tempted to look to it, rather than the biblical God, to provide ultimate meaning for life. Such challenges to Christianity must be resisted, but they are not what these verses of Scripture are talking about.

Titus 1:12

The writer of Titus, concerned about the situation of the church on the island of Crete, quotes a Cretan of earlier times, Epimenides, to the effect that "Cretans are always liars ...." That reputation was widespread in the ancient world.

But "the paradox of the Cretan liar" is of interest today in the study of logic and the search for artificial intelligence. It has connections with the theorem of Gödel which suggests that the universe cannot be, in a logical sense, a closed system. For Epimenides' statement is "self-referential" because he himself was a Cretan. If taken in the strict sense that Cretans *always* lie, he was lying when he said it, which means it's false, so he didn't have to be lying, which means it's true, so he was lying ...! It is easy to see why Epimenides' statement has been described as a "paradox."

Our text is not concerned with questions of mathematical logic, and it would be wrong to emphasize such concerns in connection with it. But it is worth nothing that the Bible speaks within the world of discourse in which these questions have been raised.[5]

James 5:13-15

This is the classic text for the practice of anointing the sick with oil as a rite of healing. We have discussed the relationship of this practice to themes of science and technology in our discussion of Mark 6:1-13 for Proper 9 B. As with the passage from Sirach 38 discussed above, this would be an excellent — one might almost say "essential" — text for a healing service. Calling attention to the common use of olive oil as medicine will help to bring out the full significance of the anointing of the sick today. Oil can be seen as a symbol of all medicines, and the rite as a prayer for divine healing through medical means.

Endnotes

1. See Cole-Turner, *The New Genesis,* for an excellent discussion of this issue.

2. E.g., "Service of the World for Healing" in *Occasional Services* (Augsburg, Minneapolis, 1982), pp. 89-98.

3. John C. Rybolt, *Sirach* (The Liturgical Press, Collegeville MN, 1986), p. 6.

4. J.N.D. Kelly, *The Pastoral Epistles* (Harper & Row, San Francisco, 1960), pp. 150-152.

5. Kelly, *The Pastoral Epistles,* pp. 235-236. Douglas R. Hofstadter, *Gödel, Escher, Bach: An Eternal Golden Braid* (Basic, New York, 1979). (References to "Epimenides paradox" are on p. 763.)

Appendix A

Index Of Texts By Season

The texts discussed in this book are listed below according to their position in the traditional church calendar. This index cross-references four major lectionaries — the *Revised Common Lectionary* (RCL) (The Consultation on Common Texts, 1992 as listed in *The Revised Common Lectionary: The Consultation on Common Texts*, Nashville: Abingdon Press, 1993); the lectionary from the *Lutheran Book of Worship* (LBW) (Minneapolis: Augsburg, 1978); and the traditional Episcopalian and Roman Catholic lectionaries. Please note that the commentaries are sequenced according to the order of the RCL. If not included in the RCL, the commentaries are sequenced as they are found in the LBW. See Appendix B for "free texts" (those not included in either the RCL or the LBW). Please note that texts which are designated as "alternate texts" in the RCL are listed below with no special designation. Texts which are common to all three years are listed below in their chronological order, except those listed at the end as "Lesser Festivals, Commemorations, and Occasions."

YEAR A

(Beginning with the first Sunday in Advent in 1995, 1998, 2001, 2004, 2007)

	Revised Common	Lutheran (1978)	Episcopal	Roman Catholic
1 Advent	Isaiah 2:1-5(6-22)	Isaiah 2:1-5(1-8/1-22)	Isaiah 2:1-5(1-8/1-22)	Isaiah 2:1-5(1-8/1-22)
3 Advent	Isaiah 35:1-10	Isaiah 35:1-10	Isaiah 35:1-10	Isaiah 35:1-10

139

	Revised Common	Lutheran (1978)	Episcopal	Roman Catholic
Christmas Day	Psalm 96, 97, 98 Isaiah 9:2-7 Luke 2:1-20 John 1:1-14 Hebrews 1:1-12	Psalm 96, 97, 98 Isaiah 9:2-7 Luke 2:1-20 John 1:1-14 Hebrews 1:1-9	Psalm 96, 97,98 Isaiah 9:2-4, 6-7 Luke 2:1-20 John 1:1-18 Hebrews 1:1-12	Psalm 96, 97, 98 Isaiah 9:1-6 Luke 2:1-20 John 1:1-14 Hebrews 1:1-9
1 Christmas	Psalm 148 Hebrews 2:10-18	Psalm 111		
2 Christmas	Sirach 24:1-12 John 1:1-18	John 1:1-18	John 1:1-18	John 1:1-18
Epiphany	Ephesians 1:3-14 Ephesians 3:1-12 Matthew 2:1-12	Ephesians 1:3-6, 15-18 Ephesians 3:2-12 Matthew 2:1-12	Ephesians 3:2-12 Matthew 2:1-12	Ephesians 3:2-12 Matthew 2:1-12
1 Epiphany	Isaiah 42:1-9	Isaiah 42:1-7	Isaiah 42:1-9	Isaiah 42:1-4, 6-7
2 Epiphany	Isaiah 49:1-7	Isaiah 49:1-6	Isaiah 49:1-7	Isaiah 49:1-7
4 Epiphany	1 Corinthians 1:18-31	1 Corinthians 1:26-31 (18-31)	1 Corinthians 1:26-31 (18-31)	1 Corinthians 1:26-31 (18-31)
5 Epiphany	1 Corinthians 2:1-16	1 Corinthians 2:1-5	1 Corinthians 2:1-11	1 Corinthians 2:1-11
6 Epiphany	Deuteronomy 30:15-20	Deuteronomy 30:15-20		
8 Epiphany	Matthew 6:24-34	1 Corinthians 2:6-13 Matthew 6:24-34	Matthew 6:24-34	1 Corinthians 2:6-13 Matthew 6:24-34
Transfiguration	2 Peter 1:16-21	2 Peter 1:16-21		2 Peter 1:16-21
Ash Wednesday	2 Corinthians 5:20—6:10	2 Corinthians 5:20—6:2	2 Corinthians 5:20b—6:10	2 Corinthians 5:20—6:10

	Revised Common	Lutheran (1978)	Episcopal	Roman Catholic
1 Lent	Genesis 2:15-17; 3:1-7	Genesis 2:7-9, 15-17; 3:1-7	Genesis 2:4b-9, 15-17; 3:1-7	Genesis 2:7-9; 3:1-7
2 Lent	Matthew 4:1-11 Romans 5:12-19 Psalm 121	Matthew 4:1-11	Matthew 4:1-11 Romans 5:12-19 Psalm 33:12-22	Matthew 4:1-11 Psalm 33
3 Lent	Romans 5:1-6 John 9:1-41	John 9:1-41	Romans 5:1-11 John 9:1-35	Romans 5:1-11 John 9:1-35
4 Lent				
Passion	Philippians 2:5-11	Philippians 2:5-11	Philippians 2:5-11	Philippians 2:5-11
Tues. of Holy Week	John 12:20-36	John 12:20-36		
Wed. of Holy Week		Romans 5:6-11		
Holy Thursday				Psalm 89 Isaiah 61:1-6 Revelation 1:4-8
Easter Vigil	Genesis 1:1—2:4a Genesis 9:8-13 Exodus 15:1-18 The Song of the Three Jews 35-65 Isaiah 25:6-9	Genesis 1:1—2:2 Genesis 9:8-13 Exodus 15:1-18 The Song of the Three Jews 35-65 Isaiah 25:6-9 Psalm 33:1-11	Genesis 1:1—2:2 Genesis 9:8-13 Exodus 15:1-18	Genesis 1:1—2:2 Exodus 15:1-18
Easter Evening				
5 Easter	John 14:1-14	John 14:1-12	John 14:1-14	Psalm 33 John 14:1-4
6 Easter	Acts 17:22-31	Acts 17:22-31	Acts 17:22-31	
Ascension	Acts 1:1-11 Ephesians 1:15-23	Acts 1:1-11 Ephesians 1:16-23	Acts 1:1-11 Ephesians 1:15-23	Acts 1:1-11 Psalm 97

	Revised Common	Lutheran (1978)	Episcopal	Roman Catholic
Vigil of Pentecost		Romans 8:14-17, 22-27	Romans 8:14-17, 22-27	
Pentecost	Psalm 104:24-34, 35b	Psalm 104:25-34	Psalm 33:12-22	Genesis 11:1-9
Trinity	Genesis 1:1—2:4a	Genesis 1:1—2:3	Psalm 104:25-37	Psalm 104
Proper 5 (June 5-11)	Psalm 33:1-12		Genesis 1:1—2:3	Psalm 104
Proper 6 (4 Pent) (June 12-18)	Romans 5:1-8(11)	Romans 5:6-11	Romans 5:6-11	Romans 5:6-11
Proper 7 (5 Pent) (June 19-25)	Romans 5:12-15	Romans 5:12-15		Romans 5:12-15
Proper 8 (June 26-July 2)	Psalm 89			Psalm 89
Proper 9 (7 Pent) (July 3-9)	Zechariah 9:9-12	Zechariah 9:9-12	Zechariah 9:9-12	Zechariah 9:9-10
				Psalm 145
Proper 10 (8 Pent) (July 10-16)	Psalm 65:1-13	Isaiah 55:10-11	Isaiah 55:1-5, 10-13	Psalm 65
	Isaiah 55:10-13	Romans 8:18-25		Isaiah 55:10-11
				Romans 8:18-25
Proper 11 (9 Pent) (July 17-23)	Isaiah 44:6-8	Isaiah 44:6-8	Romans 8:18-25	
	Romans 8:12-25			
Proper 12 (10 Pent) (July 24-30)	1 Kings 3:5-12	1 Kings 3:5-12	1 Kings 3:5-12	1 Kings 3:5, 7-12
	Matthew 13:31-33, 44-52	Matthew 13:44-52	Matthew 13:44-49a	Matthew 13:44-52
Proper 13 (11 Pent) (July 31-Aug. 6)	Psalm 145:8-9, 15-22	Psalm 104:25-31		Psalm 45
	Matthew 14:13-21	Matthew 14:13-21	Matthew 14:13-21	Matthew 14:13-21

	Revised Common	Lutheran (1978)	Episcopal	Roman Catholic
Proper 15 (Aug. 14-20)	Psalm 67			Psalm 67
Proper 16 (Aug. 21-27)	Romans 12:1-8			Romans 12:1-8
Proper 17 (15 Pent) (Aug. 28-Sept. 3)		Romans 12:1-8	Romans 12:1-8	
Proper 19 (Sept. 11-17)	Exodus 15:1b-11			
Proper 20 (Sept. 18-24)				Psalm 145
Proper 21 (Sept. 25-Oct. 1)	Psalm 19			
Proper 22 (20 Pent) (Oct. 2-8)	Philippians 3:4b-14	Philippians 3:12-21	Philippians 3:12-21	Philippians 3:12-21
Proper 23 (21 Pent) (Oct. 9-15)	Isaiah 25:1-9	Isaiah 25:6-9	Isaiah 25:1-9	Isaiah 25:6-10
Proper 24 (22 Pent) (Oct. 16-22)	Psalm 96 Matthew 22:15-22	Psalm 96 Matthew 22:15-22	Psalm 96 Matthew 22:15-22	Psalm 96 Matthew 22:15-21
Proper 25 (Oct. 23-29)	Psalm 90:1-6, 13-17			
Proper 26 (24 Pent) (Oct. 30-Nov. 5)		Amos 5:18-24		

	Revised Common	**Lutheran (1978)**	**Episcopal**	**Roman Catholic**
Proper 27 (25 Pent) (Nov. 6-12)	Amos 5:18-24	Psalm 90:12-17	Amos 5:18-24	
Proper 28 (Nov. 13-19)	Psalm 90 Zephaniah 1:7, 12-18		Psalm 90 Zephaniah 1:7, 12-18	
Proper 29 (Christ the King)	Ezekiel 34:11-16, 20-24	Ezekiel 34:11-16, 23-24		
Day of Thanksgiving	Psalm 65 Deuteronomy 8:7-18	Psalm 65 Deuteronomy 8:1-10		

YEAR B
(Beginning with the first Sunday in Advent in 1996, 1999, 2002, 2005, 2008)

	Revised Common	Lutheran (1978)	Episcopal	Roman Catholic
1 Advent	Mark 13:24-37			
2 Advent	Isaiah 40:1-11	Isaiah 40:1-11	Isaiah 40:1-11	Isaiah 40:1-5, 9-11
	2 Peter 3:8-15a	2 Peter 3:8-14	2 Peter 3:8-15a, 18	2 Peter 3:8-15a, 18
3 Advent	Isaiah 61:1-4, 8-11	Isaiah 61:1-4, 10-11		
4 Advent	Psalm 89:1-4, 19-26	Psalm 89:1-4, 14-18		
Christmas Day	Psalm 96, 97, 98	Psalm 96, 97, 98	Psalm 96, 97, 98	Psalm 89
	Isaiah 9:2-7	Isaiah 9:2-7	Isaiah 9:2-4, 6-7	Psalm 96, 97, 98
	Luke 2:1-20	Luke 2:1-20	Luke 2:1-20	Isaiah 9:1-6
	John 1:1-14	John 1:1-14	John 1:1-18	Luke 2:1-20
	Hebrews 1:1-12	Hebrews 1:1-9	Hebrews 1:1-12	John 1:1-14
				Hebrews 1:1-9
1 Christmas	Psalm 148	Psalm 111		
	Luke 2:22-40	Luke 2:25-40		Luke 2:25-40
	Sirach 24:1-12			
2 Christmas	John 1:1-18	John 1:1-18	John 1:1-18	John 1:1-18
	Ephesians 1:3-14	Ephesians 1:3-6, 15-18		
Epiphany	Ephesians 3:1-12	Ephesians 3:2-12	Matthew 2:1-12	Ephesians 3:2-12
	Matthew 2:1-12	Matthew 2:1-12		Matthew 2:1-12
1 Epiphany	Genesis 1:1-5	Isaiah 42:1-7	Isaiah 42:1-9	Isaiah 42:1-4, 6-7
2 Epiphany	Psalm 139:1-6, 13-18	Psalm 67		
	John 1:43-51			
4 Epiphany	Psalm 111		Psalm 111	

145

	Revised Common	Lutheran (1978)	Episcopal	Roman Catholic
5 Epiphany	Mark 1:29-39	Mark 1:29-39	Mark 1:29-39	Mark 1:29-39
7 Epiphany	Isaiah 43:18-25	Isaiah 43:18-25	Isaiah 43:18-25	Isaiah 43:18-25
8 Epiphany	Hosea 2:14-20	Hosea 2:14-20	Hosea 2:14-23	Hosea 2:14-23
Transfiguration	2 Corinthians 4:3-6			
Ash Wednesday	2 Corinthians 5:20—6:10	2 Corinthians 5:20b—6:2	2 Corinthians 5:20b—6:10	2 Corinthians 5:20—6:10
1 Lent	Genesis 9:8-17	Mark 1:12-15	Mark 1:9-13	Genesis 9:8-15
	Mark 1:9-15	Psalm 115		Mark 1:12-15
2 Lent	Psalm 19	Psalm 19:8-14	Psalm 19	Psalm 19
3 Lent	John 2:13-22	John 2:13-22	John 2:13-22	John 2:13-22
				1 Corinthians 1:18-31
4 Lent	Psalm 111			
5 Lent	John 12:20-33	John 12:20-33	John 12:20-33	John 12:20-33
Passion	Philippians 2:5-11	Philippians 2:5-11	Philippians 2:5-11	Philippians 2:5-11
Tues. of Holy Week	John 12:20-36	John 12:20-36		
Wed. of Holy Week		Romans 5:6-11		
Holy Thursday				Psalm 89
				Isaiah 61:1-6
				Revelation 1:4-8
Easter Vigil	Genesis 1:1—2:4a	Genesis 1:1—2:2	Genesis 1:1—2:2	Genesis 1:1—2:2
	Genesis 9:8-13	Genesis 9:8-13	Genesis 9:8-13	
	Exodus 15:1-18	Exodus 15:1-18	Exodus 15:1-18	Exodus 15:1-18
	The Song of the Three Jews 35-65	The Song of the Three Jews 35-65		

	Revised Common	Lutheran (1978)	Episcopal	Roman Catholic
Easter Day	Isaiah 25:6-9	Isaiah 25:6-9	Isaiah 25:6-9	
Easter Evening	Isaiah 25:6-9	Isaiah 25:6-9		
2 Easter		Psalm 148		
3 Easter		Psalm 139		
6 Easter	Psalm 98	Psalm 98	Psalm 98	Psalm 98
Ascension	Acts 1:1-11	Acts 1:1-11	Psalm 33	Acts 1:1-11
	Ephesians 1:15-23	Ephesians 1:16-23	Acts 1:1-11	Ephesians 1:16-23
		Romans 8:14-17, 22-27	Ephesians 1:15-23	Romans 8:14-17, 22-27
Vigil of Pentecost			Romans 8:14-17, 22-27	Genesis 11:1-9
				Psalm 104
				Psalm 104
				Psalm 33
				Romans 8
Pentecost	Romans 8:22-27	Psalm 104	Psalm 104:25-37	
Trinity	Psalm 139			
Proper 4 (2 Pent)	2 Corinthians 4:5-12	2 Corinthians 4:5-12	2 Corinthians 4:5-12	2 Corinthians 4:5-12
(May 29-June 4)	Genesis 3:8-15	Genesis 3:9-15	Genesis 3:8-21	Genesis 3:9-15
Proper 5 (3 Pent)				
(June 5-11)				
Proper 6 (4 Pent)	Psalm 20			
(June 12-18)	2 Corinthians 5:6-10			
	(11-13) 14-17			
	2 Corinthians 6:1-11			
Proper 7 (5 Pent)	Psalm 107:1-3, 23-32	Psalm 107:1-3, 23-32	Psalm 107:1-3, 23-32	Psalm 107
(June 19-25)	Job 38:1-11	Job 38:1-11	Job 38:1-11	
	2 Corinthians 5:14-21	2 Corinthians 5:14-21	2 Corinthians 5:14-21	2 Corinthians 5:14-21
	Mark 4:35-41	Mark 4:35-41	Mark 4:35-41	Mark 4:35-41

	Revised Common	Lutheran (1978)	Episcopal	Roman Catholic
Proper 8 (6 Pent) (June 26-July 2)	Mark 5:21-43	Mark 5:24b-34	Mark 5:22-34	Mark 5:22b-34
Proper 9 (July 3-9)	Mark 6:1-13			
Proper 10 (8 Pent) (July 10-16)	Ephesians 1:3-14	Ephesians 1:3-14 Mark 6:7-13	Ephesians 1:3-14 Mark 6:7-13	Ephesians 1:3-14 Mark 6:7-13
Proper 12 (10 Pent) (July 24-30)	Psalm 145:10-18 John 6:1-21	Psalm 145 John 6:1-15		Psalm 145 John 6:1-15
Proper 15 (13 Pent) (Aug. 14-20)	Psalm 111 Proverbs 9:1-6 John 6:51-58	Proverbs 9:1-6 John 6:51-58	Proverbs 9:1-6 John 6:53-59	Proverbs 9:1-6 John 6:51-58
Proper 16 (Aug. 21-27)	1 Kings 8:(1, 6, 10-11) 22-30 Ephesians 6:10-20			
Proper 17 (15 Pent) (Aug. 28-Sept. 3)		Ephesians 6:10-20	Ephesians 6:10-20	
Proper 18 (16 Pent) (Sept. 4-10)	Isaiah 35:4-7a Mark 7:24-37	Isaiah 35:4-7a Mark 7:31-37	Isaiah 35:4-7a Mark 7:31-37	Isaiah 35:4-7 Mark 7:31-37
Proper 20 (18 Pent) (Sept. 18-24)	James 3:13—4:3, 7-8a	James 3:16—4:6	James 3:16—4:6	James 3:13-18
Proper 21 (19 Pent) (Sept. 25-Oct. 1)		James 4:7—5:6	James 4:7—5:6 Hebrews 2:(1-8) 9-18	Psalm 19
Proper 22 (20 Pent) (Oct. 2-8)	Psalm 8			Hebrews 2:10-18

	Revised Common	Lutheran (1978)	Episcopal	Roman Catholic
Proper 23 (21 Pent) (Oct. 9-15)	Psalm 90:12-17 Amos 5:6-7, 10-15	Psalm 90 Amos 5:6-7, 10-15	Psalm 90 Amos 5:6-7, 10-15	Psalm 90 Wisdom 7:7-14
Proper 24 (22 Pent) (Oct. 16-22)	Psalm 104:1-9, 24, 35c Job 38:1-7 (34-41)			Psalm 33
Proper 25 (23 Pent) (Oct. 23-29)	Mark 10:46-52	Mark 10:46-52	Mark 10:46-52	Mark 10:46-52
Proper 26 (24 Pent) (Oct. 30-Nov. 5)	Deuteronomy 6:1-9 Ruth 1:1-18	Deuteronomy 6:1-9	Deuteronomy 6:1-9	Deuteronomy 6:1-9
Proper 27 (25 Pent) (Nov. 6-12)	Hebrews 9:24-28	Hebrews 9:25-28	Hebrews 9:24-28	Hebrews 9:24-28
Proper 28 (27 Pent) (Nov. 13-19)	Mark 13:1-8	Psalm 111 Mark 13:24-31		
Christ the King (Proper 29)	John 18:33-37 Revelation 1:4b-8	John 18:33-37 Revelation 1:4b-8	John 18:33-37 Revelation 1:4-8	Mark 13:24-32 John 18:33-37 Revelation 1:4-8

YEAR C

(Beginning with the first Sunday in Advent in 1997, 2000, 2003, 2006)

	Revised Common	Lutheran (1978)	Episcopal	Roman Catholic
1 Advent	Luke 21:25-36	Luke 21:25-36		Luke 21:25-36
2 Advent	Malachi 3:1-4	Malachi 3:1-4		
Christmas Day	Psalm 96, 97, 98	Psalm 96, 97, 98	Psalm 96, 97, 98	Psalm 96, 97, 98
	Isaiah 9:2-7	Isaiah 9:2-7	Isaiah 9:2-4, 6-7	Isaiah 9:1-6
	Luke 2:1-20	Luke 2:1-20	Luke 2:1-20	Luke 2:1-20
	John 1:1-14	John 1:1-14	John 1:1-14	John 1:1-14
	Hebrews 1:1-12	Hebrews 1:1-9	Hebrews 1:1-12	Hebrews 1:1-9
1 Christmas	Psalm 148	Psalm 111		Hebrews 2:14-18
		Hebrews 2:10-18		Luke 2:11-52
2 Christmas	Luke 2:41-52	Luke 2:41-52		
	Sirach 24:1-12			
	John 1:1-18	John 1:1-18	John 1:1-18	John 1:1-18
Epiphany	Ephesians 1:3-14	Ephesians 1:3-6, 15-18		
	Ephesians 3:1-14	Ephesians 3:2-12	Ephesians 3:2-12	Ephesians 3:2-12
	Matthew 2:1-12	Matthew 2:1-12	Matthew 2:1-12	Matthew 2:1-12
1 Epiphany	Isaiah 43:16-21	Isaiah 42:1-7	Isaiah 42:1-7	Isaiah 42:1-4, 6-7
2 Epiphany	Psalm 36:5-10	Psalm 36:5-10		Psalm 96
3 Epiphany		Isaiah 61:1-6		Psalm 19
	1 Corinthians 12:12-31a	1 Corinthians 12:12-21, 26-27	1 Corinthians 12:12-31	1 Corinthians 12:12-31
4 Epiphany	Jeremiah 1:4-10	Jeremiah 1:4-10	Jeremiah 1:4-10	
		1 Corinthians 12:27—13:13		

	Revised Common	**Lutheran (1978)**	**Episcopal**	**Roman Catholic**
7 Epiphany	1 Corinthians 15:35-38a, 42-50	1 Corinthians 15:35-38a, 42-50	1 Corinthians 15:35-38a, 42-50	1 Corinthians 35-38a, 42-50
8 Epiphany	Isaiah 55:10-13			
9 Epiphany	Psalm 96			
	Luke 7:1-10			
Transfiguration		2 Corinthians 4:3-6		
Ash Wednesday	2 Corinthians 5:20—6:10	2 Corinthians 5:20—6:2	2 Corinthians 5:20b—6:10	2 Corinthians 5:20b—6:10
1 Lent	Deuteronomy 26:1-11	Deuteronomy 26:5-10	Deuteronomy 26:5-11	Deuteronomy 26:5-11
2 Lent	Philippians 3:17—4:1	Philippians 3:17—4:1	Philippians 3:17—4:1	Philippians 3:17—4:1
4 Lent		1 Corinthians 1:18-31		
5 Lent	Isaiah 43:16-21	Isaiah 43:14-21	Isaiah 43:16-21	Isaiah 43:16-21
Passion	Philippians 2:5-11	Philippians 2:5-11	Philippians 2:5-11	Philippians 3:12-21
Tues. of Holy Week	John 12:20-36	John 12:20-36		Philippians 2:5-11
Wed. of Holy Week		Romans 5:6-11		
Holy Thursday				Psalm 89
				Isaiah 61:1-6
				Revelation 1:4-8
Easter Vigil	Genesis 1:1—2:4a	Genesis 1:1—2:2	Genesis 1:1—2:2	Genesis 1:1—2:2
	Genesis 9:8-13	Genesis 9:8-13	Genesis 9:8-13	Exodus 15:1-18
	Exodus 15:1-18	Genesis 15:1-18	Exodus 15:1-18	
	The Song of the Three Jews 35-65	The Song of the Three Jews 35-65		
Easter Day		Exodus 15:1-11		

	Revised Common	Lutheran (1978)	Episcopal	Roman Catholic
Easter Evening	Isaiah 25:6-9	Isaiah 25:6-9		
2 Easter	Revelation 1:4-8	Revelation 1:4-8	Revelation 1:1-8	
3 Easter	Revelation 5:11-14	Revelation 5:11-14	Revelation 5:6-14	
5 Easter	Psalm 148		Psalm 95	Psalm 95
	Revelation 21:1-6	Revelation 21:1-5	Acts 14:8-18	Revelation 21:10-14, 23-27
6 Easter	Psalm 67	Acts 14:8-18		Psalm 67
	Revelation 21:10, 22—22:5	Revelation 21:10-14, 22-23	Revelation 21:10-14, 22-27	Revelation 21:10-14, 22-27
Ascension	Acts 1:1-11	Acts 1:1-11	Acts 1:1-11	Acts 1:1-11
	Ephesians 1:15-23	Ephesians 1:16-23	Ephesians 1:15-23	Ephesians 1:16-23
Vigil of Pentecost		Romans 8:14-17, 22-27	Romans 8:14-17, 22-27	Genesis 11:1-6
				Psalm 104
Pentecost	Psalm 104:24-34, 35b	Psalm 104:25-34	Psalm 104:25-37	
	Genesis 11:1-9	Genesis 11:1-9	Genesis 11:1-9	
	Romans 8:14-17, 22-27		Romans 8:14-17, 22-27	
Trinity	Psalm 8	Psalm 8		Psalm 8
	Proverbs 8:1-4, 22-31	Proverbs 8:22-31		Proverbs 8:22-31
	Romans 5:1-5			
Proper 4 (2 Pent)	Psalm 96			
(May 29-June 4)	1 Kings 8:22-23, 41-43	1 Kings 8:22-43	1 Kings 8:22-43	1 Kings 8:22-43
	Luke 7:1-10	Luke 7:1-10	Luke 7:1-10	Luke 7:1-10

	Revised Common	Lutheran (1978)	Episcopal	Roman Catholic
Proper 5 (3 Pent) (June 5-11)	1 Kings 17:17-24 Luke 7:11-17	1 Kings 17:17-24 Luke 7:11-17	1 Kings 17:17-24 Luke 7:11-17	1 Kings 17:17-24 Luke 7:11-17
Proper 10 (8 Pent) (July 10-16)				Colossians 1:13-20
Proper 12 (10 Pent) (July 24-30)	Colossians 2:6-15 (16-19)	Colossians 2:6-15	Colossians 2:6-15	Colossians 2:6-15
Proper 13 (11 Pent) (July 31-Aug. 6)	Ecclesiastes 1:2, 12-14, 2:18-23	Ecclesiastes 1:2, 2:18-26	Ecclesiastes 1:2, 2:18-26	Ecclesiastes 1:2, 21-23
Proper 14 (12 Pent) (Aug. 7-13)	Psalm 33:12-22	Psalm 33	Psalm 33	Psalm 33
Proper 15 (13 Pent) (Aug. 14-20)	Jeremiah 23:23-29	Jeremiah 23:23-29	Jeremiah 23:23-29	
Proper 16 (Aug. 21-27)	Jeremiah 1:4-10			
Proper 18 (16 Pent) (Sept. 4-10)	Psalm 139:1-6, 13-18	Proverbs 9:8-12		Psalm 90
Proper 19 (17 Pent) (Sept. 11-17)				Amos 8:4-7
Proper 20 (18 Pent) (Sept. 18-24)	Amos 8:4-7	Amos 8:4-7	Amos 8:4-7	
Proper 23 (21 Pent) (Sept. 25-Oct. 1)	Psalm 111 2 Kings 5:1-3, 7-15c Luke 17:11-19	Psalm 111 Ruth 1:1-19a Luke 17:11-19	Ruth 1:1-19a Luke 17:11-19	Psalm 98 Luke 17:11-19

	Revised Common	Lutheran (1978)	Episcopal	Roman Catholic
Proper 24 (22 Pent) (Oct. 16-22)	Psalm 121	Psalm 121	Psalm 121	Psalm 121
Proper 25 (Oct. 23-29)	Psalm 65			Psalm 145
Proper 26 (24 Pent) (Oct. 30-Nov. 5)	Psalm 98	Psalm 148		
Proper 27 (25 Pent) (Nov. 6-12)	Luke 20:27-38	Luke 20:27-38		Luke 20:27-38
Proper 28 (26 Pent) (Nov. 13-19)	Psalm 98			Psalm 98
Christ the King (Proper 29)	Colossians 1:11-20	Colossians 1:13-20	Colossians 1:11-20	Colossians 1:11-20
Day of Thanksgiving	Deuteronomy 26:1-11	Psalm 65		

LESSER FESTIVALS, COMMEMORATIONS AND OCCASIONS

	Lutheran	Episcopal	Roman Catholic
Saint Andrew	Psalm 19	Psalm 19	Psalm 139
Saint John	Genesis 1:1-5, 26-31		Jeremiah 1:4-10
The Name of Jesus	Psalm 8		
Saint Mark	Psalm 57		
Nativity of Saint John the Baptist	Malachi 3:1-4		
Saint Bartholomew	John 1:43-51		
	1 Corinthians 12:27-31a		
Holy Cross Day	Isaiah 45:21-25	Isaiah 45:21-38	
	Psalm 98	Psalm 98	
	John 12:20-33	John 12:20-33	
	1 Corinthians 1:18-24		
Commemoration of Saints	1 Corinthians 1:26-31 (18-31)	1 Corinthians 1:26-31 (18-31) (III)	
Commemoration of Theologians	Wisdom 7:7-14	Wisdom 7:7-14 (I)	
	Matthew 13:47-52	Matthew 13:44-52 (II)	
	1 Corinthians 2:6-10, 13-16	1 Corinthians 2:6-13 (I)	
Commemoration of Artists and Scientists	Matthew 13:44-52		
	Psalm 96		
Dedication and Anniversary	1 Kings 8:22-30		
Harvest	Deuteronomy 26:1-11		
	Psalm 65		

	Lutheran	Episcopal	Roman Catholic
National Holiday	Psalm 20		
Peace	Micah 4:1-5	Micah 4:1-5	
Stewardship of Creation	Job 39:1-11, 16-18 Psalm 104:1, 13-24 or 25-37		
New Year's Eve	Psalm 102		
Saint Joseph			Psalm 89
All Souls			Psalm 115 John 14:1-12

Appendix B
Index Of Texts By Books Of The Bible

The texts discussed in this book are listed below according to their position in the biblical canon. This index cross-references two major lectionaries — the *Revised Common Lectionary* (RCL) (The Consultation on Common Texts, 1992 as listed in *The Revised Common Lectionary: The Consultation on Common Texts,* Nashville: Abingdon Press, 1993) and the lectionary from the *Lutheran Book of Worship* (LBW) (Minneapolis: Augsburg, 1978). Please note that the commentaries are sequenced according to the order of the RCL and are listed here according to the RCL. If not included in the RCL, the commentaries are listed as they are found in the LBW (1978). A few free texts are also listed. Please note that texts which are designated as "alternate texts" in the RCL are listed below with no special designation. In some cases, specific verses of some frequently used Psalms are not listed.

	Revised Common	**Lutheran**
Genesis		
1:1—2:4a	Easter Vigil	Easter Vigil
	Trinity A	Trinity A
	1 Epiphany B	
1:1-5, 26-31		Saint John
2:(7-9) 15-17; 3:1-7	1 Lent A	1 Lent A
3:8-15	Proper 5 B	3 Pentecost B
9:8-17	Easter Vigil	Easter Vigil
	1 Lent B	
11:1-9	Pentecost C	Pentecost C
Exodus		
15:1-18	Easter Vigil	Easter Vigil
		Easter C
	Proper 19 A	
31:1-11 (free text)		
Leviticus		
25:1-24 (free text)		

157

	Revised Common	**Lutheran**
Deuteronomy		
6:1-9	Proper 26 B	24 Pentecost B
8:(1-18) 7-18	Day of Thanksgiving A	Day of Thanksgiving ABC
26:1-11	Day of Thanksgiving C	Harvest
	1 Lent C	
26:5-10		1 Lent C
30:15-20	6 Epiphany A	6 Epiphany A
Ruth		
1:1-18	Proper 26 B	21 Pentecost C
1 Kings		
3:5-12	Proper 12 A	10 Pentecost A
8:(1, 6, 10-11) 22-30	Proper 16 B	Dedication & Anniversary
8:22-43	Proper 4 C	2 Pentecost C
17:17-24	Proper 5 C	3 Pentecost C
2 Kings		
5:1-3, 7-15c	Proper 23 C	
Job		
28:20-28 (free text)		
38:1-11	Proper 7 B	5 Pentecost B
	Proper 24 B	
39:1-11, 16-18		Stewardship of Creation
Psalm		
8	Trinity C	Trinity C
	The Name of Jesus ABC	The Name of Jesus ABC
	New Year ABC	
	Proper 22 B	
19	3 Lent B	3 Lent B
	Easter Vigil ABC	Saint Andrew
	3 Epiphany C	
	Proper 22 A	
	Proper 19 B	
20	Proper 6 B	National Holiday
		4 Pentecost B

	Revised Common	**Lutheran**
33	Proper 5 A	5 Easter A
	Proper 14 C	12 Pentecost C
36:5-10	2 Epiphany C	2 Epiphany C
57		Saint Mark
61:1-4, 8-11	3 Advent B	
65	Proper 10 A	Harvest
	Day of Thanksgiving	Day of Thanksgiving
	Proper 25 C	
67	6 Easter C	2 Epiphany B
	Proper 15 A	
89:1-4, 19-26	4 Advent B	4 Advent B
	Proper 8 A	
90	Proper 28 A	21 Pentecost B
90:1-6, 13-17	Proper 25 A	
90:12-17	Proper 23 B	25 Pentecost A
96	Proper 24 A	22 Pentecost A
	Christmas ABC	Christmas ABC
	Proper 4 C	Comm. of Artists &
	9 Epiphany C	Scientists
97	Christmas ABC	Christmas ABC
98	Christmas ABC	Christmas ABC
	6 Easter B	6 Easter B
	Proper 27 C	Holy Cross Day
	Proper 28 C	
102		New Year's Eve
104	Proper 24 B	Pentecost B
104:25-34	Pentecost AC	Pentecost AC
		11 Pentecost A
		Stewardship of Creation
107:1-3, 23-32	Proper 7 B	5 Pentecost B
111	4 Lent B	1 Christmas ABC
	4 Epiphany B	27 Pentecost B
	Proper 15 B	
	Proper 23 C	21 Pentecost C
115		2 Lent B
121	Proper 24 C	22 Pentecost C
	2 Lent A	
135		19 Pentecost B

	Revised Common	**Lutheran**
139	2 Epiphany B	3 Easter B
	Proper 4 B	
	Proper 18 C	
145	Proper 13 A	10 Pentecost B
	Proper 12 B	
	Proper 27 C	
148	1 Christmas ABC	2 Easter B
	5 Easter C	25 Pentecost C

Proverbs

8:1-4, 22-31	Trinity C	Trinity C
9:1-6	Proper 15 B	13 Pentecost B
9:8-12		16 Pentecost C

Ecclesiastes

1:2, 12-14, 2:18-23	Proper 13 C	11 Pentecost C

Isaiah

2:1-5 (6-22) (free text)	1 Advent A	1 Advent A
9:2-7	Christmas ABC	Christmas ABC
25:6-9	Easter Evening ABC	Easter Evening ABC
	Easter Day B	21 Pentecost A
	Proper 23 A	
35:1-10	3 Advent A	3 Advent A
35:4-7a	Proper 18 B	16 Pentecost B
40:1-11	2 Advent B	2 Advent B
42:1-9	1 Epiphany A	1 Epiphany ABC
43:16-21	1 Epiphany C	
	7 Epiphany B	7 Epiphany B
	5 Lent C	5 Lent C
44:6-8	Proper 11 A	9 Pentecost A
45:21-38		Holy Cross Day
49:1-7	2 Epiphany A	2 Epiphany A
55:10-13	8 Epiphany C	8 Pentecost A
	Proper 10 A	
61:1-6	3 Advent B	3 Epiphany C
		3 Advent B

	Revised Common	**Lutheran**
Jeremiah		
1:4-10	4 Epiphany C	4 Epiphany C
	Proper 16 C	
23:23-29	Proper 15 C	13 Pentecost C
Ezekiel		
34:11-16, 20-24	Christ the King A	Christ the King A
Hosea		
2:14-20	8 Epiphany B	8 Epiphany B
Amos		
5:6-7, 10-15	Proper 23 B	21 Pentecost B
5:18-24	Proper 27 A	24 Pentecost A
8:4-7	Proper 20 C	18 Pentecost C
Micah		
4:1-5		Peace
Zephaniah		
1:7, 12-18	Proper 28 A	
Zechariah		
9:9-12	Proper 9 A	7 Pentecost A
Malachi		
3:1-4	2 Advent C	2 Advent C
		Nativity of Saint John the Baptist
Wisdom		
7:7-14		Comm. of Theologians
7:7-22 (free text)		
Sirach		
24:1-12	2 Christmas ABC	
38:1-15 (free text)		
The Song of the Three Jews		
35-65	Easter Vigil	Easter Vigil

	Revised Common	**Lutheran**
Matthew		
2:1-12	Epiphany ABC	Epiphany ABC
4:1-11	1 Lent A	1 Lent A
6:24-34	8 Epiphany A	8 Epiphany A
13:31-33, 44-52	Proper 12 A	10 Pentecost A
		Comm. of Theologians
		Comm. of Artists and Scientists
14:13-21	Proper 13 A	11 Pentecost A
22:15-22	Proper 24 A	22 Pentecost A
Mark		
1:9-15	1 Lent B	1 Lent B
1:29-39	5 Epiphany B	5 Epiphany B
4:35-41	Proper 7 B	5 Pentecost B
5:21-43	Proper 8 B	6 Pentecost B
6:1-13	Proper 9 B	8 Pentecost B
7:24-37	Proper 18 B	16 Pentecost B
10:46-52	Proper 25 B	23 Pentecost B
13:24-37	1 Advent B	27 Pentecost B
Luke		
2:1-20	Christmas ABC	Christmas ABC
2:22-40	1 Christmas B	1 Christmas B
2:41-52	1 Christmas C	1 Christmas C
7:1-10	Proper 4 C	2 Pentecost C
	9 Epiphany C	
7:11-17	Proper 5 C	3 Pentecost C
17:11-19	Proper 23 C	21 Pentecost C
20:27-38	Proper 27 C	25 Pentecost C
21:25-36	1 Advent C	1 Advent C
John		
1:1-14	Christmas ABC	Christmas ABC
1:1-18	2 Christmas ABC	2 Christmas ABC
1:43-51	2 Epiphany B	Saint Bartholomew
2:13-22	3 Lent B	3 Lent B
6:1-15	Proper 12 B	10 Pentecost B
6:51-58	Proper 15 B	13 Pentecost B

	Revised Common	**Lutheran**
9:1-41	4 Lent A	3 Lent A
12:20-36	5 Lent B	5 Lent B
	Tues. of Holy Week ABC	Tues. of Holy Week ABC
		Holy Cross Day
14:1-14	5 Easter A	5 Easter A
18:33-37	Christ the King B	Christ the King B

Acts
1:1-11	Ascension ABC	Ascension ABC
14:8-18		6 Easter C
17:22-31	6 Easter A	6 Easter A

Romans
5:1-8 (11)	Trinity C	4 Pentecost A
	Proper 6 A	
5:6-11	3 Lent A	Wed. of Holy Week ABC
		4 Pentecost A
5:12-19	1 Lent A	5 Pentecost A
8:14-17, 22-27	Pentecost BC	Vigil of Pentecost ABC
8:12-25	Proper 11 A	8 Pentecost A
12:1-8	Proper 16 A	15 Pentecost A

1 Corinthians
1:26-31 (18-31)	4 Epiphany A	4 Epiphany A
		Commemoration of Saints
		4 Lent C
		Holy Cross Day
2:1-16	5 Epiphany A	5 Epiphany A
2:6-13	5 Epiphany A	6 Epiphany A
		Comm. of Theologians
12:12-31a	3 Epiphany C	3 Epiphany C
		Saint Bartholomew
12:27—13:13		4 Epiphany C
15:35-38a, 42-50	7 Epiphany C	7 Epiphany C

2 Corinthians
4:3-6	Transfiguration B	Transfiguration C
4:5-12	Proper 4 B	2 Pentecost B
5:20b—6:10	Ash Wednesday ABC	Ash Wednesday ABC
	Proper 7 B	

	Revised Common	**Lutheran**
Ephesians		
1:3-14	Proper 10 B	8 Pentecost B
	2 Christmas ABC	2 Christmas ABC
1:15-23	Ascension ABC	Ascension ABC
3:1-12	Epiphany ABC	Epiphany ABC
6:10-20	Proper 16 B	15 Pentecost B
Philippians		
2:5-11	Palm/Passion ABC	Passion ABC
	Holy Name ABC	
3:4b-14 (21)	Proper 22 A	20 Pentecost A
3:17—4:1	2 Lent C	2 Lent C
Colossians		
1:13-20	Christ the King C	Christ the King C
2:6-15	Proper 12 C	10 Pentecost C
1 Timothy		
6:20-21 (free text)		
Titus		
1:12 (free text)		
Hebrews		
1:1-12	Christmas ABC	Christmas ABC
2:10-18	1 Christmas A	1 Christmas C
9:24-28	Proper 27 B	25 Pentecost B
James		
3:13—4:3, 7-8	Proper 20 B	
4:7—5:6		19 Pentecost B
5:13-15 (free text)		
2 Peter		
1:16-21	Transfiguration A	Transfiguration A
3:8-15a	2 Advent B	2 Advent B
Revelation		
1:4b-8	2 Easter C	2 Easter C
	Christ the King B	Christ the King B
5:11-14	3 Easter C	3 Easter C
21:1-6	5 Easter C	5 Easter C
21:10-14, 22—22:5	6 Easter C	6 Easter C

Appendix C
Major Topics In Preaching About Science And Technology From The Lectionary

Most of the texts discussed in this book fall into a few major categories which represent issues and themes related to the intersection of science, technology and faith. We have not tried to be exhaustive or definitive in the creation of categories or the placement of texts within the categories. Neither are the categories meant to be mutually exclusive. Rather, the diversity represented by the categories is meant to suggest the variety of ways the biblical tradition can be approached for the purpose of preaching at the intersection of science, technology and faith. In some cases, the relationship between a particular text and one of the following topics is direct, explicit and far-ranging. In other cases the relationship is marginal and limited. In *all* cases, our purpose is to encourage the preacher to seek out themes in the biblical witness which speak to and illuminate our lives in an age of science and technology, or to bring contemporary insight to the task of understanding and articulating the biblical witness for our lives. This is what it means to be a *cosmic witness*.

A list of the texts in each category can be found at the end of this appendix. The categories and subcategories include:

> God And The Cosmos
> > Cosmology
> > Creation
> > Natural Theology
> > Wholistic View of the Universe/Creation
> > Valuing the Natural World
> > Miracles and Science

Human Being And Responsibility
   Science, Technology and Human Vocation
   Appropriate Technology
   Idolatry and Hubris

Wisdom, Knowledge, Truth And Authority

Scientific Metaphors, Analogies Or Explanations

Technological Metaphors

God And The Cosmos

The texts included in the broad category of **God and the Cosmos** generally deal with questions and issues about God's relationship to the universe — the context of our "worldly," "empirical" or "natural" existence. This section is divided into several subsections, each of which focuses on some aspect of the relationship of God and the universe, or on how we in the Judaeo-Christian tradition have attempted to grapple with the nature and implications of this relationship.

Cosmology (from the Greek, *kosmos*, meaning world or universe) is the philosophical or astrophysical study of the origins, processes and structures of the universe. Cosmology intersects theology and faith by raising questions about origins, processes and structures of the universe in light of theological principles and religious values, ideas and ideals. Many of the texts discussed in this book provoke consideration of cosmology by providing a comparison of biblical cosmologies with modern scientific and philosophical positions. In this book we recognize that this comparison should be considered a two-way street. Not only can contemporary science and philosophy be used to "demythologize" the biblical traditions, but biblical insight must be allowed to challenge our "modern," science-based comprehension and experience of the world. The texts listed in this category in *Appendix C* provide a range of insights into various biblical cosmologies, as well as an introduction to many of the questions which have challenged, confronted and frustrated human beings for millennia.

The texts of the second subsection of **God and the Cosmos** deal explicitly with the notion of **Creation**, particularly with the image of God as the **Creator**. The preacher is challenged to see creation expressed not only in terms of the processes which brought the universe into being, but also the capacity of the universe to continue to be created and creating.

Natural Theology has been, and continues to be, an influential way of comprehending the relationship of God and the cosmos. This third subsection includes some of the scriptural references which are frequently associated with natural theology. Our purpose, however, is not to attempt to defend or reject natural theology. Rather, we highlight these texts so that they might be used by the preacher to explore the range of issues raised by natural theology, including the question of what role natural theology should play in contemporary theology and faith.

The texts associated with the notion of a **Wholistic View of the Universe/Creation** present the universe as something which ought to be comprehended and valued in its unity. They reject the suggestion that "human" existence is essentially *other than*, or necessarily *better than,* the world of nature. This set of texts works in conjunction with those included in **Valuing the Natural World** to provoke the need to relativize human being in relationship to other aspects of existence. Together, the texts of those two subcategories can provide an often-lacking sense of humility and other-centeredness on the part of humanity.

Miracle stories have often stood at the center of controversies between science and religion. The lectionary readings which comprise the **Miracles and Science** subsection provide the preacher a context to explore these controversies, and to develop a means by which we who live in an age of science and high-technology can encounter the breadth and depth of the biblical witness, including those truths and insights which are embodied in these miracle stories.

Human Being And Responsibility

The category of **Human Being and Responsibility** focuses on the human dimension of existence. Here it is helpful to think of science and technology as modes of human activity. Science is the extension or enhancement of human knowledge and understanding of the physical universe. Likewise, technology is the extension or enhancement of human capacity and power by artificial means. Considering science and technology as forms of human activity allows us to approach the biblical witness for insight into this aspect of the human condition.

In the section called **Science, Technology and Human Vocation**, we encounter texts which explore these modes of human being as a calling or vocation, established by God, to be fulfilled by God's people. These texts also depict the character of human *responsibility* for the products and processes of human endeavor, including those related to science and technology. The challenge for the preacher is to explore how notions of vocation and responsibility found within the biblical witness can be appropriated in our time, even with respect to human activities which persons in biblical times could never have imagined, even in their wildest dreams.

The category of **Appropriate Technology** includes texts which suggest that certain forms of technological activity may or may not correspond to God's will for humanity or God's purposes in creation. These texts are sometimes associated with prophetic visions of the "Day of the Lord," when destruction is replaced by nurture (symbolized in Isaiah 2, for instance, with the turning of swords into plowshares). Other texts refer to common time, when our technological (and scientific) activity is, nevertheless, to be judged as being appropriate in God's sight. Often, in such cases, appropriateness refers to the ideals of justice or peace. Taken as a whole, these texts can be used to preach about morally justifiable technology in the present day.

Related to the notions of vocation, responsibility, and appropriateness are the issues of **Idolatry and Hubris** (sinful pride) in relation to science and technology. The texts in this section portray our predilection to pay homage to some of the more awesome and powerful products of human endeavor. They also provide a means for the preacher to underscore our human tendency to try to use science and technology to "make a name for ourselves" (Genesis 11:4, the story of Babel), to attempt to be like God.

Taken as a whole, texts within the categories related to human being and responsibility allow the preacher to focus on both positive and negative features of life in a scientific and technological age. From portraying a sense of vocation, to warning of the temptation to idolatrous and prideful behavior, these texts can help to illuminate the human condition at the intersection of science, technology and faith.

Wisdom, Knowledge, Truth And Authority

Whereas many of the texts related to **Human Being and Responsibility** focused on technology, the texts in the category of **Wisdom, Knowledge, Truth and Authority** are predominately associated with science. The preacher can use these texts to juxtapose science and *wisdom* — wisdom as understood in the so-called "wisdom tradition" of ancient Judaism. Biblical insights into *knowledge* and *truth* can also be examined in light of the claims of modern science. Likewise, science can be viewed through the lens of the biblical witness to examine the limits and possibilities of science to incorporate Truth. Finally, these texts also afford the preacher an opportunity to jump headlong into the "faith/science debate" by raising the issue of **authority**.

Scientific Metaphors, Analogies Or Explanations

We have included several texts to illustrate how **scientific metaphors, analogies and explanations** can be used to illuminate the biblical witness. Several branches of science are used, including the "social" or "behavioral" sciences (see Isaiah 61:1-6 and Mark 1:29-39). Among the scientific concepts, principles, and theories we have used in this book are:

Maxwell's equations of electromagnetism, relativity, the wave theory of light, evolution, genetics, the second law of thermodynamics, quantum mechanics, and mathematical symmetry. We include a brief description of the scientific concepts, principles, and theories which have been used to illustrate each text in this category.

The purpose of these illustrations is threefold. First, the use of such illustrations indicates the valid application of science to the understanding of existence, including existence as it is portrayed in the biblical witness. Second, this affords us the possibility to encourage preachers to incorporate science into the life of the Church (especially among those for whom science is "not their thing"). Third, this may inspire those within the Church with a science background (both lay and clergy) to bring the distinctive and powerful insights of contemporary science to the preaching ministry of the Church.

Use of certain scientific concepts, principles, and theories in this fashion does not constitute an endorsement of any particular interpretation of Scripture or Tradition. Rather, the use of these particular scientific metaphors, analogies and explanations are offered as imaginative and effective ways to illuminate the biblical witness for our time.

Technological Metaphors

Our final category of texts are those which involve the use of **technological metaphors**. Generally, these metaphors — such as the prophetic use of "planting and keeping" — emerge from the biblical witness itself. The preacher's task is to explore how to use these metaphors both to illustrate the biblical witness for persons immersed in a technological way of life, and to examine ways these metaphors can be used to examine this technological way of life theologically and morally.

Index Of Texts By Topic

GOD AND THE COSMOS

Cosmology

Genesis 1:1—2:4a
Deuteronomy 6:1-9
1 Kings 8:22-43
Job 38:1-11
Psalm 8
Psalm 19
Psalm 89:1-4, 19-26
Psalm 96
Psalm 97
Psalm 98
Psalm 111
Psalm 121
Psalm 139
Psalm 148

Proverbs 8:1-4, 22-31
Jeremiah 23:23-29
Amos 5:6-7, 10-15
Mark 13:24-37
Luke 2:22-40
John 1:1-18
1 Corinthians 1:26-31 (18-31)
Ephesians 1:3-14
Ephesians 6:10-20
Colossians 1:13-20
James 4:7—5:6
Revelation 5:11-14
Revelation 21:1-6

Creation

Genesis 1:1—2:4a
Genesis 9:8-17
Deuteronomy 26:5-10
1 Kings 8:22-43
Job 38:1-11
Psalm 33
Psalm 67
Psalm 89:1-4, 19-26
Psalm 104:25-34
Psalm 107:1-3, 23-32
Psalm 111

Psalm 115
Psalm 139
Psalm 145
Isaiah 43:16-21
Mark 4:35-41
Luke 7:11-17
Romans 8:12-25
2 Corinthians 5:6-17
Ephesians 1:3-14
Colossians 2:6-15
Hebrews 1:1-12

Natural Theology

Psalm 8
Psalm 19
Proverbs 9:8-12
Matthew 14:13-21

John 9:1-41
Acts 14:8-18
Acts 17:22-31
Colossians 2:6-15

Wholistic View Of The Universe/Creation

Deuteronomy 8:(1-18) 7-18
Psalm 96
Psalm 104:25-34
Hosea 2:14-20

1 Corinthians 12:12-31a
Philippians 2:5-11
Hebrews 2:10-18

Valuing The Natural World

Isaiah 25:6-9
Isaiah 35:1-10
Hosea 2:14-20
Amos 5:6-7, 10-15
Luke 2:22-40

John 2:13-22
1 Corinthians 12:12-31a
Philippians 3:4b-14 (21)
Hebrews 9:24-28

Miracles And Science

Matthew 14:13-21
Mark 1:29-39
Mark 7:24-37
Mark 10:46-52
Luke 7:1-10

Luke 7:11-17
John 6:1-15
John 6:51-58
James 4:7—5:6

HUMAN BEING AND RESPONSIBILITY

Science, Technology And Human Vocation

Genesis 1:1—2:4a
Genesis 2:7-9, 15-17, 3:1-7
Genesis 3:9-15
Genesis 11:1-9
Psalm 90:12-17
Psalm 115
Isaiah 42:1-9
Isaiah 43:16-21
Isaiah 45:21-38
Isaiah 49:1-7
Isaiah 61:1-6

Jeremiah 1:4-10
Amos 5:18-24
Zephaniah 1:7, 12-18
Malachi 3:1-4
Matthew 6:24-34
Matthew 13:44-52
Matthew 14:13-21
Matthew 22:15-22
Mark 7:24-37
Luke 2:22-40
Romans 8:12-25

Appropriate Technology

Genesis 2:7-9, 15-17, 3:1-7
Genesis 3:9-15
Genesis 11:1-9
Deuteronomy 30:15-20
1 Kings 3:5-12
Psalm 20
Psalm 90:12-17
Psalm 115
Proverbs 9:8-12
Isaiah 2:1-5 (6-22)
Isaiah 9:2-7
Isaiah 35:1-10
Isaiah 45:21-38
Isaiah 49:1-7
Isaiah 61:1-6
Jeremiah 1:4-10
Amos 5:6-7, 10-15
Amos 5:18-24
Micah 4:1-5
Zephaniah 1:7, 12-18
Zechariah 9:9-12
Matthew 14:13-21
Matthew 22:15-22
Romans 8:12-25
Ephesians 6:10-20

Idolatry And Hubris

Genesis 3:9-15
Genesis 11:1-9
1 Kings 3:5-12
Psalm 20
Psalm 90:12-17
Psalm 115
Isaiah 2:1-5 (6-22)
Jeremiah 1:4-10
Zephaniah 1:7, 12-18
Zechariah 9:9-12
Ephesians 6:10-20

WISDOM, KNOWLEDGE, TRUTH AND AUTHORITY

Genesis 1:1—2:4a
1 Kings 3:5-12
Job 28:20-28
Job 39:1-11, 16-18
Psalm 121
Proverbs 9:8-12
Ecclesiastes 1:2, 12-14, 2:18-23
Isaiah 49:1-7
Wisdom 7:7-14
Matthew 2:1-12
Mark 7:24-37
Luke 2:22-40
John 6:51-58
John 18:33-37
1 Corinthians 2:1-16
1 Corinthians 2:6-15
Ephesians 6:10-20
Colossians 2:6-15
James 3:13—4:3, 7-8
2 Peter 1:16-21

SCIENTIFIC METAPHORS, ANALOGIES OR EXPLANATIONS
Genesis 1:1—2:4a (evolution)
Ruth 1:1-18 (biology of race)
Psalm 8 (anthropic principle, scientific cosmology)
Psalm 36 (light)
Psalm 65 (nuclear processes)
Psalm 148 (anthropic principle)
Ecclesiastes 1:2, 12-14, 2:18-23 (scientific skepticism)
Isaiah 55:10-11 (laws of nature)
Isaiah 61:1-6 (evolution, family systems theory)
Amos 5:6-7, 10-15 (evolution, scientific cosmology)
Matthew 4:1-11 (recapitulation, evolution)
Mark 1:12-15 (recapitulation, evolution)
Mark 1:29-39 (laws of nature, role of mind in healing process)
John 1:1-18 (rationality, quantum field theory, anthropic principle)
John 14:1-12 (speed of light)
Acts 1:1-11 (relativity/space-time)
Romans 5:6-11 (genetics, evolution)
Romans 5:12-15 (genetics, evolution)
Romans 8:12-25 (second law of thermodynamics, evolution)
Romans 12:1-8 (evolution)
1 Corinthians 12:12-31a (evolution)
1 Corinthians 15:35-38a, 42-50 (biology of life and death, atomic [quantum] theory)
2 Corinthians 4:5-12 (Maxwell's equations of electromagnetism)
2 Corinthians 5:20—6:2 (time)
Ephesians 1:3-14 (anthropic principle, evolution)
Colossians 1:13-20 (anthropic principle, evolution)
Colossians 2:6-15 (nature of science, scientific claims to truth)
Hebrews 2:10-18 (evolution)
Hebrews 9:24-28 (mathematical symmetry)
James 4:7—5:6 (wave theology of light, "Poisson's Spot")
2 Peter 3:8-14 (evolutionary time scale)

TECHNOLOGICAL METAPHORS
Genesis 3:9-15 (tilling and keeping)
Psalm 90:12-17 (building and planting)
Jeremiah 1:4-10 (building and planting)
Amos 8:4-7 (weights and measures)
Zephaniah 1:7, 12-18 (building and planting)
Malachi 3:1-4 (craft/metallurgy)
Mark 5:24b-34 (medicine)
Mark 6:7-13 (medicine)
Mark 10:46-52 (medicine)

Appendix D
Technology And Justice

The language of just, sustainable, and participatory technology comes from the work of the World Council of Churches, which has provided a broad-based forum for theological analysis of technology. According to Roger Shinn, the WCC's program on technology can be traced to a 1966 consultation on Church and Society: Christians in the Social and Technical Revolutions of Our Time. Soon thereafter, heightened concern over the ecological crisis focused attention within the WCC on a wide spectrum of social problems related to life in the technological age. At the 1975 World Assembly, a call was issued to the Christian community which set the agenda for a major effort within the WCC for the next several years.

The responsibility that now confronts humanity is to make

> *a deliberate transition to a sustainable global society in which science and technology will be mobilized to meet the basic physical and spiritual needs of people, to minimize human suffering and to create an environment which can sustain a decent quality of life for all people. This will involve a radical transformation of civilization, new technologies, new uses for technology and new global economic and political systems. The new situation in which humanity now finds itself has been created in less than a generation. There is even less time to create the transition to a sustainable global society if humanity is to survive.* (Quoted in Garrison Lee, John Loonman, and Robert Parsonage, "Consultation Inaugurates Year Long Process," *Faith, Science, and Technology Forum* [Education in the Society, National Council of Churches of Christ, New York, 1983], p. 1.)

Growing interest within the WCC culminated in the 1979 "Faith, Science, and the Future" conference, held at The Massachusetts Institute of Technology (MIT).

The MIT conference brought together a wide range of theological, ecclesiastical, scientific, and technical expertise. For a bibliographic summary of materials related to this conference, see:

Mitcham and Grote, *Theology and Technology: Essays in Christian Analysis and Exegesis* (Lanham, Md.: University Press of America, 1984), pp. 329-331.

The WCC has published three books which chronicle the conference's multifaceted debate.

Paul Abrecht, ed., *Faith, Science, and the Future* (Philadelphia: Fortress Press, 1979).

Roger L. Shinn, ed., *Faith and Science in an Unjust World,* vol. 1, *Plenary Presentations* (Philadelphia: Fortress Press, 1980).

Paul Abrecht, ed., *Faith and Science in an Unjust World,* vol. 2, *Reports and Recommendations* (Philadelphia: Fortress Press, 1980).

The first includes a series of articles by the organizing committee which set the agenda for the activities of the conference. The two subsequent volumes summarize the work of the various conference subgroups, offering conclusions and suggestions for further study or action by the WCC, its member churches, and scholars.

Appendix E

Story Sermons

These two science fiction story sermons are intended to suggest an imaginative way of preaching. They are not expositions of their texts, parts of the First Lesson for Christ the King A and the Gospel for 1 Lent B. But they do develop hints in these texts in ways which address some modern concerns.

Hope In Heaven

Eighty years out from earth, the ship crept between the stars. Though it would achieve a tenth of light speed, another century and a half would pass before its journey ended. Three miles long, the ship was a little world to itself.

Juanita Lopez walked slowly along the corridor. Usually friendly, today she hardly noticed the people she met. Her inner eye was fixed on the baby in the ship's clinic, the baby who should not have been born. Now the decision was hers as the ship's chief medical officer: genetic contamination or purity? Life or death?

She came almost automatically to her destination, the small building in the park where she could think quietly. There was seldom anyone there. Some called it "the chapel," though it had no official name. Many people back on earth had opposed sending any sign at all of religion on the first voyage to the stars, and no preference could be shown to any of earth's faiths. So the chapel was simply a plain room with a few chairs and symbols on its walls — the star of David, the calm Buddha, and others. It was the calmness that helped when she had problems to solve or decisions to make. The Yin-Yang flow or the purity of the Zoroastrian flame spoke in mysterious ways of a hope for peace.

Juanita sank into a chair and thought back to the clinic. She couldn't forget the look of that baby — not quite normal, but so close that nothing had been noticed at first. They simply had assumed that all the prenatal tests would catch any problems, and of course all of the shippers had to have a clean genetic record. All the old hereditary diseases were supposed to be history. Her assistant, Jack Williams, had done some careful detective work to track down the difficulty.

"A small error in the DNA," he said, looking at the computer screen. "Might be from the increased cosmic radiation, though we can't be sure. There were no obvious physical signs. The chemical tests from amniocentesis should have picked it up, but somehow we missed it. Maybe we've gotten overconfident."

"It may be a small error," she said, "but the child's development shows severe brain deficiencies — what they called mental retardation back on earth. And there could be physical problems as well."

"Yes," said Jack. "It shouldn't have been born. And now, at six months . . . ."

His voice had trailed off, but Juanita knew what he meant. Could they put a child that age to death? But could it be allowed to live? What kind of sign would that be for the shippers? For generations they had learned that people have a right to genetic health and a duty to maintain it. This wasn't a decision she wanted to make. Doctors were supposed to save life. And they were supposed to ensure that all lives were healthy.

Life had been so different on earth. How much simpler their decisions must have been! She opened her eyes and looked around the chapel. Like most of the shippers, she had gotten only the vaguest ideas about the old religions — a few comments in school, or odds and ends in conversations. But she thought now how comforting it must have been to think that there was some benevolent God up in heaven taking care of things. How easy to have such a God who would always tell you what decisions to make! But now the ship was travelling through the heavens, and all that was left of those old beliefs were these ancient symbols. At least they were able to give her an irrational sense of peace and security.

All but the one she didn't like to look at.

It was a man nailed to a piece of wood, his bleeding body twisted in pain. It was bad enough to have to see those few in the clinic who were sick or hurt. But this! Someone had told her that this was supposed to be *God*. God abandoned, suffering, and dying. There was no peace and security there.

God thrown away by society? God killed? This man nailed to the wood?

If there were a God (just suppose), then would any life be without hope? Would even death be hopeless? (You're in interstellar space, Juanita! We recycle the bodies of our dead, so that none of the valuable chemicals will be wasted. This is no place for myths.) Was this lonely, dying man supposed to be a sign of *hope*? For whom?

For me, destined to die and have my body reduced to atoms light years from home?

For a damaged baby whose life seems pointless in this little bubble of health creeping between the stars? What seems pointless to me would be no barrier to that God on the wood (if there is any God).

Why should a scientist, of all people, think that answers could always be easy?

She rose to go, to act. Peace seemed a long way off, but it might be real peace.

> *For thus says the Lord GOD: I myself will search for my sheep, and will seek them out. As shepherds seek out their flocks when they are among their scattered sheep, so I will seek out my sheep. I will rescue them from all the places to which they have been scattered on a day of clouds and thick darkness.* — Ezekiel 34:11-12

Time Travel

The Spirit hurled Jesus into the desert. Fresh from the joy and exaltation of his baptism, fresh from hearing the heavenly voice which said, *"You are my beloved Son"* — just when he was coming up out of the water, the Spirit seized Jesus and drove him into the wilderness. He could hardly move fast enough to keep up — running, walking to catch his breath. Out — away from people, away from villages, into the rocky open spaces. He went back to where his fathers and mothers had lived centuries before. Back to the wandering in the wilderness, back — for forty days, always farther back, and farther away.

It was, as the Book says, *"The howling waste of the wilderness."* There was nothing there but rock and sand. Nothing but the hot winds of the day and the cold winds of the night, and the sounds and cries of the desert beasts — the birds, the crawling things. The birds circling high overhead and the snakes slithering across the rock. Always back.

He awoke in the long ago. He was clothed in skins and furs that scratched and smelled bad, but didn't keep the icy wind out very well. He sat beside a small fire where a few chunks of the woolly mammoth's flesh were roasting. His few companions were exhausted after the violent hunt which had ended with two of them dead. They had had enough to eat for the first time in weeks, and were full and sleepy. The rest of them were snoring loudly. A cold wind blew down from the ice fields a few miles to the north, bearing more snow.

Then he heard a snuffling sound, and looked out into the darkness. Soon a single scrawny wolf appeared at the edge of the firelight. It must have been starving to come close to humans; it must have smelled the food. Maybe it had followed the trail of blood from the hunt.

Without thinking, he had reached for his spear. The message in his brain had been automatic: Beast — enemy — kill. Humans had to kill wolves, just as wolves always had to kill humans. He gripped the spear. But then he stopped and looked at the starving wolf. The beast did not look at him. It was gazing at the pieces of uncooked meat that lay on the rock beside him. And he thought, "It's hungry, too — just the way we were yesterday."

Very slowly, he speared a piece of the meat, and very slowly he reached it out to the beast. The wolf just watched, but its tongue hung out. The man lowered the dripping meat from the end of his spear to the ground. The wolf approached, slowly, warily — then suddenly seized the chunk and raced out of the firelight. But the next night he was back, at the edge of the darkness. And this time he approached the man a little more quickly, and came a bit nearer.

But that would be too late. He had to go farther back.

He crouched behind a tree — one of a small group of trees on the vast rolling plains of Africa. A few other humans crouched beside him, hidden as if in wait for game. They clutched stones which had been chipped to make rough hand axes. Beasts were coming.

These were the beasts that they hated, not just the ones they hunted for food. These were beasts that looked like humans, and who walked erect like humans — but they were just beasts. They were different from humans.

The beasts who walked erect looked like humans at a distance. But up close their skins were seen to be pale, and their foreheads were more sloped. They had no hand axes — only sharp sticks. And the grunts they made to each other were different from the grunts of the humans. They were different. They were beasts who had fought with the humans before. They had to be killed.

Now the beast people were coming quietly through the grass, each one looking carefully for edible roots or perhaps some bird eggs or a lizard for food. They were so intent on their search that they did not pick up the scent of the humans, crouched behind the trees. Quickly, at his command, the humans surrounded the beasts-who-looked-human, the fists bearing their axes raised. Sharpened sticks were raised in defiance.

And then, before he could give the command to strike, he happened to look into the eyes of one of the beast people. He saw there the same hate, the same fear, that he had seen in the eyes of his people — in the eyes of humans. The eyes into which he looked were strange in color and shape, but they were human eyes. Slowly, he lowered his fist. His people looked questioningly at him and grunted, "Kill? Kill?" But no one moved. Then the stranger in front of him slowly lowered his spear and looked at him. Carefully, deliberately, he dropped his axe to the ground. He held out his hands, palms up. The stranger held his spear level for a moment and tensed his muscles — then dropped it and held out his hands.

But that would be too late. He had to go farther back.

A hundred million years ago, no humans walked the earth. The dinosaurs ruled the world. The huge hundred-foot-long *brontosaurus* placidly chewed the tops of the trees; the terrible carnivore *tyrannosaurus rex,* "tyrant lizard king," ran down its prey on its two hind legs like some caricature of a human, tearing apart whatever it caught with teeth like butcher knives.

Humans had not yet evolved. But this human walked along a path in the garden in the shade of the trees, looking for some fruit for a midday meal. He passed one tree in the center of the garden and saw that its fruit was ripe and beautiful — but of course *that* tree was out of bounds. He started to walk on.

Suddenly a huge form reared up and stepped out into the open beside that special tree. It was *tyrannosaurus rex.* The tyrant lizard looked down at the little human, and bent its huge head down, and opened its jaws with those butcher-knife teeth — and spoke.

"This is a beautiful tree, isn't it?" asked the dinosaur.

"Yes, it is," said the human.

"Mmm — beautiful fruit, too. Looks as if it's just ripe for picking. If I weren't carnivorous, I'd probably eat some." Then *tyrannosaurus* paused. "Tell me," it went on, "is it really true that God told you not to eat from *any* tree of the garden?"

"No," said the human. "Just from this one. *'In the day that you eat of it, you shall surely die.'* "

"Uh-huh," said the tyrant. "I see. That's interesting. You know — I'll bet you wouldn't really *die* if you ate some of this fruit! That's probably kind of an exaggeration, don't you think?" The human said nothing.

"In fact, probably nothing would happen if you ate some of this fruit. God just wants to be able to give you an order — *any* order — and have you obey it. Kind of to keep you in your place, you know. And so if you did eat — you'd be just as good as God. It would be like saying you could tell right from wrong yourself, without any arbitrary rules. God wants to keep you toeing the line, but you can make your own decisions."

The man looked at the tree and looked at the beautiful fruit and said, "No." And he started to walk on.

"Wait a minute, wait a minute," yelled *tyrannosaurus,* and loped after the human. It jumped onto the path in front of him.

"Look," said the dinosaur, its voice no longer so friendly. "Perhaps I didn't make myself clear. Maybe you don't understand who I am. I'm the king. I rule this world. Nobody defies me. God can give all the orders he likes, but I'm the one who has the power here. If you know what's good for you, you'll go back and eat some of that fruit!" Then the dinosaur voice, with an effort, became friendly again: "Be reasonable. You're hungry and ..."

"No," said the man, and walked on.

"You'll never get away with this," the tyrant screamed after him. "Nobody disobeys the king! I'm not finished with you yet!"

Jesus turned around and smiled grimly, smiled for the first time in forty days. And then he walked forward.

"And the angels came to him."
— Mark 1:12-15 (RSV)